HALTING STEPS

# HALTING STEPS

## Collected and New Poems

# CLARIBEL ALEGRÍA

CURBSTONE BOOKS

NORTHWESTERN UNIVERSITY PRESS

EVANSTON, ILLINOIS

Curbstone Books
Northwestern University Press
www.nupress.northwestern.edu

Printed in the United States of America

10  9  8  7  6  5  4  3  2  1

**Library of Congress Cataloging-in-Publication Data**
Alegría, Claribel.
   [Poems. English]
   Halting steps : collected and new poems / Claribel Alegría.
     p. cm.
   In English, translated from the Spanish.
   ISBN 978-0-8101-2919-1 (pbk. : alk. paper)
   I. Title.
  PQ7539.A47A2 2013
  861.64—dc23

                         2013004356

♾ The paper used in this publication meets the minimum requirements of the American National Standard for Information Sciences—Permanence of Paper for Printed Library Materials, ANSI Z39.48-1992.

*To Sandy Taylor*

# CONTENTS

*Otherness* (2011)

HALTING STEPS

# RING OF SILENCE
## (1948)

*Translated from the Spanish by*
*Margaret Sayers Peden*

# High Are the Pillars

Tall are the columns of my dream,
moving toward the song on bare feet,
they issue from somewhere deep within me
and spiral upward on the wind.

Sometimes I surprise them among the clouds,
In the golden afternoons, in the stars,
they linger in everything that's beautiful
and continue their illuminated voyage.

How delicate are the columns of my dream!
I almost confuse them with the mist,
I can't see them anymore, anguish, shadows . . .
I fear that they will fall and break!

No, they can't fall, they reach toward the song,
To the song that is theirs and awaits them!
They issue
from somewhere deep within me
and spiral upward on the wind!

# To My Mother

Someone is knocking at the door.
It's life waiting, pulsing with yearning,
life inviting me to see the world
from the unbound grace of its open arms.

I'm leaving, Mother, I'm leaving.
I want to feel the emotion of the instant,
get drunk with joy at the starry night,
and speak to pain without your knowing.

I'm not forgetting anything. It's late.
I will bring you garlands of hyacinth,
In my skirts I will gather the gold of stars
and from my lips you will see the song rise.

Good-bye Mother, don't cry.
Don't stop me, I am going with life.

# Let Me Come In

Let me come into your grief,
I won't break the silence.
I will take fresh roses for scent
And my love like a lantern.

For your dark skies
I have the fire of stars,
birds aflame
and kingdoms of white clouds.

Let me come in,
I'll wait until you open for me.
I am alone in the shadows
and the whirling of wind bites.

## Bold Wind

Stop chasing me,
Bold wind of the North,
leave me, I want to rest,
I want to lie down in the fields.

Do you want my silk ribbon?
Do you want my ring, my brooch?
Take them wind but let me go
I want to be alone in the forest.

I have run and run
From day to night!
I jumped rivers in my flight
and crossed horizons.

Stop chasing me,
Bold wind of the North;
Leave me, I want to rest,
I want to lie down in the forest.

# A Spring

Hidden in the night there is a spring
my sleepless heart has told me,
nearby the music of water
and a scent of magnolias in the air.

Come, let's look for it among the leaves.
I want to get drunk with its white grace,
I want to moisten my lips in its waves
and wash my secret in its foam.

Let's run until we come upon its banks,
don't let the moon get ahead,
I want to see myself in its flowing
and sing with it as the day dawns.

# Come See the Rain

Don't close the door,
come see the rain jumping and skipping,
come and see the rain falling from the depths of the sky
and setting its song afire on the wind.

I feel something beautiful today,
as if a tremor was rising to my lips from within
and wants to reveal wise words
and dance, dance with the white rain giving its secret
to the world.

I am bewitched listening to what the rain is telling me!
everything is shivering outside,
everything in suspense waiting for the ominous sign.

Open the windows,
look at the rain running barefoot across the earth.

# LOVE SONNETS
## (1953)

*Translated from the Spanish by*
*Margaret Sayers Peden*

## 1

From what distant and blazing height
did love descend to knock at my door?
It surged naked from the silent shadow and
at the dawn there was sweetness on my lips.

The word, permeated with happiness,
is in my blood a warm and open flower.
An archangel that awakens in my veins
and erases all bitterness from my voice.

I am bound to the masthead of its ship
by the green caress of the ocean depths.
On the edge of its voice leaps the key

that held the anguish of my verse.
For it I rock the world in my arms
and breathe in a rose the universe.

## 2

Let us celebrate, Love, this joy
as together we look from the window,
and hear at the same time the bell
that with its song announces a new day.

With the first light of dawn
all things are born anew in harmony.
Even though I feel so much a human
there is something celestial in my joy.

Open my heart, it is there that shadow,
in a corner purified by sadness,
shelters its nocturnal designs.

But look well. Go down to the depths.
In a hidden pool, the deepest of the deep,
the rivulet of my life flows clear.

# 3

How shall I sing to you, Love, sing
that shiver left by your caress?
High peaks of delight
and my voice trembles with happiness.

From my bones rises news of you
and spreads through all body.
The blood in my veins unhinges
lodging its anxiety in my throat.

When I think of your miraculous dance
that fulfills the presence of the rose
and opens extravagant fields of color,

I want you to know, Love, that you cleanse me,
that your trembling inflames my tasks
but my word withdraws in the night.

4

You are, beloved, the everyday angel
that comes to me in the good and the bad.
You watch over my waking hours, and appear
in my sleep like the midday sun.

You lead me by the hand through the world
and smooth the wrinkles from my brow.
Sculptor of my song, sweet master
whose footsteps announce the summer.

You have made celestial the custom
of bolting the doors at night
and lighting the dawn with our love.

For you my solitude is resplendent,
the light of my eyes is clear
and the best of all moments is now.

# 5

I want to tell you, beloved, the poetry
given us in the bread, the bed, the song,
the audacious spring, the sweet weeping
of the child awaking to the day.

It tastes of winter earth, of distance,
the name that covers us with its mantle.
In my hours of shadow and of tears
it is a lily that lights my desert.

For all these reasons I love you.
The way you talk, your eyelids, your stature,
the grace of your gentle movements

as you lay your body down like a river.
When the sea closes me within dark night,
it is your voice that captains my ship.

# 6

Your serenity gives me such pleasure,
as well as that expression you hide
in a dark zone of your feelings, and
though typical of you, it is foreign to me.

It is the humble gesture of a good man
and it fills oblivions with songbirds.
It restores my injured heart
and transforms all venom into love.

Sometimes you lose love and it does not
come out to light your face with its aroma
of clear mountains or country fields.

And I welcome it with joy,
when in your eyes it glimpses me
and roses are born from my human shadow.

# 7

Wait, Love. Wait for me patiently
beside the quiet ardor of your wakefulness.
Wait for me to come, lifting to the sky
the jovial banner of your smile.

I shall attack you, lightly, imprecisely,
amid the ripe aroma of the plum,
in the stone smoothed by the stream,
among the deep currents of the breeze.

When I come back to you it will be without tears,
with summers rising from my song
and innocence instilled upon my lips.

I want to love you again with sweet fervor,
inflamed with sun in fields of gold,
with no dark abysses in my awareness.

# 8

Love's time passes by without hours.
It is as clean as the air in springtime.
At the clear signal of its banner
dawns will robe themselves in dew.

Love lights the things you don't know,
pointing out to you grain in the meadow,
the stone of a long mountain range
and a wall covered with climbing vines.

Everything ends in its embrace. Nothing forgets.
Love is a lamp in the night. In its reflection
every rose is a favorite rose.

Don't let it escape. Come back, beloved.
We will be reborn in it. In its retinue
figures of the past are alive and dancing.

# 9

With my most recent, my naked voice,
I will teach your name to a rose garden,
to the dawn wind in fields of wheat,
and to the dreams of climbing ivy.

Because your lineage is of love and it protects
the shorelines will tell it to the sea.
From hearing it so long in many forms
even mute stone will learn your name.

I will shout it now that it is summer,
beneath the brilliant, transfiguring sun
that high above is entirely mine.

Mine, like your kiss, the fecund seed
from which the flower will be born,
is what my body senses within me.

# Elegy for a Sailor

Your heartbeat lay in the silent sea,
your exiled, wandering sailor's voice.
Like the wind that announces the coming storm
my wakened sorrow stirred, and shook.

It is now seven years. I can't forget.
I sense your footstep in the morning star,
in the hidden bend of the forest path,
in the heather that evokes your name.

So winged, so soaring, my sense of you!
But in that doleful clime of emptiness,
naught but the memory of my wound.

I call with my old voice but there is no answer.
Your throat, your words, are hidden in the sea
and in it my heart finds no repose.

# Sunday's Monologue

Five o'clock in the afternoon.
What will I do with the joy that runs through my veins?
I don't like this room.
It has four walls that hide the light.
I will go out and seek the sun
and people will see me starred with songs,
falling over myself,
escaping,
detached from time.
I have a comb, a handkerchief and the key.
That's all I need.
The stairs creak when I jump.
Poor, lonely things that stay behind in the house,
under the dark embrace of silence.
Why that strange gesture?
(A mocking grimace brushing past my face.)
It smells of Sundays.
The trees seem taller
and joyfully dance to the wind.
There's a gray cloud.
The cloud will pass by.
I want a clear, illuminated sky,
like the image of my soul.
This afternoon my soul is out to party.
The sun looks down at me, it looks down and blushes.
The porter's eyes!
The porter's eyes!
What do you want of me? I was going to ask him,
but the stubborn words died on my lips.
The tramway lights up with noises.
How it drags its glory through the streets!

How they wait for it to come!
The tramway smells of rotten fruit and sweat.
I'll get off now.
The eyes of the porter!
Just forget him.
Greens, whites, violets, reds.
The group of doves anoint the afternoon with love.
A pregnant woman perpetuates the landscape.
The sky is cloudy!
Will it rain?
The porter, the porter.
Where have I seen him before?
His thin lips pressed together,
his yellow skin
and his gold ring.
So many people in the streets.
I'll walk to the north,
Where the city ends sooner.
Houses . . . shops . . . houses . . .
A circle of children in the park.
The grass has grown
and envelops them with love.
Listen to the shoes on the sidewalk.
Clap, clap, clap.
They feel tired.
The horizontal foot
like dreams and earth.
How soon it has grown dark.
Not one star in the sky.
The wind blows
And slides down my body.
Who said night was maternal?
Everything rolls to emptiness.
Not one star in the sky,
not one corner in the soul illuminated.
This is the street, yes.

6a Avenida Sur.
The roofs are leaking.
The walls tattooed with tears.
Night closes in on me.
How scratched up the house!
Among all the houses, the oldest.
Nailed to the door are the eyes.
The knocker stutters in the hallway.
My knees tremble.
Someone is coming, someone
like through a tunnel.
The door slowly opens.
Who hides there and looks at me?
It's his face, his face.
One shiver, another one.
No. Not to my room.
I'll go to the kitchen and warm my feet.
No, better my room.
The shaky wail of the stairs.
Did someone knock?
Eyes don't dare look back.
Where's the key?
I've lost the key.
No.
The room is empty.
The rug so dirty!
In my face his gray and distorted gesture.
What a hungry look when he extends his hand,
the look of a haughty beggar.
I guess, I guess.
He dressed up as a porter
and lies in wait at entrances
and exits.
Maybe tonight is the night.
How, my God?
I am afraid. I am alone.

The paths, the rivers,
wait for me in their arms.
I have an old date
with the rosebush in the park,
with the lilacs and the ceiba
and the delicate spiderweb.
You're looking for me. Yes. You're looking for me.
I can smell your breath.
I don't want to wake up in your darkness,
further than the hours.
Is it time to run away?
Through the back door, without making noise.
I'll leave my shoes.
Everything, I'll leave everything.
Again the stairs.
The hallway seems full of fingernails.
Whose shadow is in the patio?
Something moved!
But there's no one, no one.
My blood freezes.
What a long trip with no return.
As stingy as he might be,
a corner in the world.
The door opens.
I'm wrong.
It has opened and creaks and I haven't reached it.
(It's your sneering grimace brushing my face.)
Defeat announces me.
I can't leave, no.
I shall stay in your house
and go up the stairs running.

# AQUARIUS
# (1955)

*Translated from the Spanish by*
*Margaret Sayers Peden*

# Aquarius

It was only a gesture.
And I was afraid.
I hugged my knees
and held on tight to my world,
to that world of light that surrounds us.
And again I was afraid.
It's perilous to live in an aquarium,
exposed to gazes,
to acid rocks
thrown by neighbors,
to words of yours or maybe mine
that cloud it
or break it.

That is all I have left
to be able to look at the world without suspicion.
Only that, my Aquarius,
to soften the blows
and give me the measure
of all those who leave
and return to their sea,
and of those who lose their way
and die on the dunes.
My one refuge,
do you understand?
And it is so easy to destroy it.

# Midpoint of the Journey

Sometimes we would like to start over.
Pick up the dangling threads
we left years ago
and follow the design in a different pattern.
I took the wrong door so many times,
and went in
and was alone,
and other times didn't go in
because I couldn't.
And in the middle of the landscape
nostalgia frequently assaults me
and I am forsaken,
and I remember windows
and smiles,
and I go on by.

It is futile to think of going back.
I will follow at a slower pace,
and when the day comes to tie knots
I will be able to look back
and perhaps find an unexpected design.

# This Mirror Understands Me

I will arrive at night,
after the bolts have been shot,
after the parties and prayers.

I know the streets well,
I remember them,
with their scent of summer
and peacefulness.
I have not been able to keep
my rendezvous with the ceiba
and now I feel this solitude
in my knees
and it buckles them.

From my door I see
processions of shadows.
and voices are echoes,
and the wind is an obtuse
profile on the street corners.

I will go back to my city
where the simple faces of the houses
invite us to come in.

This mirror understands me.
I am going to look for my image
in things over there.

# Walking This Afternoon

I need to tell you of my happiness.
Walking this afternoon I realized:
I am not dragging chains.
My body is agile,
with no skin to oppress it.
Numbers do not assault me in front of the bank
and I give my heart to the one I want.

Why burden myself with wealth
and things less urgent than bread
if the lakes of the south belong to me,
and the Izalco volcano,
and the ceiba awaiting my arrival?

Today life is buzzing in my ears
and nipping my back
its warmth flowing through my eyes.
Where is my love so I can tell him?

# Letter to Time

Dear Sir:
I write this letter on my birthday.
I received your gift. I don't like it.
It is always the same.

As a girl I waited impatient;
I dressed up and went to the street
to talk about it.

Don't be stubborn.
I can still see you playing
chess with my grandfather.
At first your visits were rare.
Soon they became daily
and Grandfather's voice
lost its luster.
And you insisted
without respect for his humility,
his gentle soul, his shoes.

Later you courted me.
I was still young
and you with your unchanging face.
A friend of my father's
with one eye on me.

Poor Grandfather.
You waited at his deathbed for the end.
The walls paled
and there was someone else.
An unknown air

floated among the things in the room.
You called to him
and he closed my grandfather's eyes
and looked at me.

I forbid you to come back.
Each time I see you my spine stiffens.

Stop following me.
I beg you.
It has been years since I have loved another
and your gifts are no longer of interest.

Why do you wait for me in shopwindows,
in sleep's mouth,
beneath the uncertain Sunday sky?
Your greeting tastes of musty rooms.

I saw you the other day with the children.
I knew your suit, the same tweed
when you were my father's friend
and I was a student.
Your ridiculous autumn suit.

Do not come back.
I insist.
Do not linger in my garden.

The children will frighten
and the leaves drop.
I have seen them.

What is the use of all of this?

You will laugh a while
and with that unending laugh
you will still turn up.
The children,
my face,
leaves,
all nothing in your eyes.
You will win.
I knew it when I began.

# Adaptations

Every day I am accompanied by
the refrigerator,
the stove,
and their set angles
make my eyes sad.

I know some people
with spoon faces,
and others who group together
like plates
and polish their smiles
and shatter them to bits.
And bored couples
whose color is slowly fading
and who will never find each other.
And men who encircle their void
with impenetrable barbed wire.

Sometimes it occurs to me
that it is easy to be an armoire
and let yourself be filled with spiderwebs,
or a door that others open
and close at their whim,
or a shelf of books
and dust.

I could give up
and turn into a utensil.
But always there is the sea,
and the hearth
and clover
sending its aroma my way,
and I stray off path.

# I Was Born Here Too

I left.
My hour had come.
But I didn't leave completely;
my greens all stayed.
Each time I come back I breathe them.

Later I left again
from many places.
I never leave completely.
But that isn't a bad deal.
I arrive an invited guest
and accumulate riches.

No one can take from me
my encounters,
my conversations,
my faces.

What difference does it make whether
I leave or stay?
I was born here too.

# Personal Profile

I am four feet nine.
Chestnut eyes.
Will I dare to laugh,
to ask questions,
to destroy the armor they've put on me
and to scream from shame?

I know how to read and write,
but I've not been able to put aside my grudges.
I was never in jail.
What's the point of so many signs and countersigns
if it's more difficult to know each other now than before?
Every night I am pained by what I've said.
In dreams I wear a disguise.

I play an absurd part
and have forgotten the script.
A number identifies me
and I am dying of thirst.

But in spite of it all the song emerges,
and at customs they don't know what to do
so they let it come out.

# GUEST OF MY TIME
## (1960)

*Translated from the Spanish by*
*Margaret Sayers Peden*

# Home Movie

I have a surprise for you.
In just a few minutes
you will be seeing your face on the screen.

The technician's arrived.
Yes, he's here.
Smelling a little of whiskey
and a whiff of tobacco.
Everything's ready.
Come in.
Up to the highest seats,
so intimate,
so cold.

My father as a boy.
Looking for seashells
and his world.
I have lost my sense of wonder
and can't find it.
I smell of mildew.

The air,
the outdoor air,
I can take it in a capsule.
It goes very slowly, *señora*.
That's natural,
you get bored.
What does it have to do with our lives?

My father has stopped
walking slowly
and barely pauses at shopwindows.
Instead of seashells,
newspapers,
abrupt movements,
flights.

Maestro, for God's sake
what are you laughing at?
Can't you stop just one moment
in my childhood?
I was looking for jasmine.
When did the scent change to gasoline?

Do you recognize yourself, Lola?
We have only an empty shell
left of her.
Would she still be able to feel nostalgic?
Here I am, again,
feeling the stress of childhood.

And that burning ship
and that scene of war?
Faster and faster.

I comb my hair in ringlets
and think, timidly,
of love.

You're mistaken, maestro.
That doesn't concern us.
Your laughing distracts us.
What do I care about that ulcer
like a flower on the screen?

And that woman, what is she doing
with her face buried in her hands?
Wind the film back,
I beg you.
But here you are, children,
all of you.
Everything is a flickering, chaotic
whirlpool.

Faster and faster.
The images are melting together.
Shadows are fluttering on the screen.
It snapped.
Darkness,
stumbling,
and an alcoholic laugh of good-bye.

# Journey's Eve

Today I took a long walk around Valparaíso.
Over a cup of coffee
I talked with you,
with you whom I haven't seen for so long.

In these boringly sensitive days
I am a series
of muffled explosions,
collapses,
fresh cement.
With every step I trip over tastes,
over smells that block my path.

As I am packing the porcelain
I think about Friday night:
the figure of Salvador
dancing the tango,
how shy Manolo was.

Which of my memories will be broken on arrival?
There is a crack they escape through,
the crack where I continuously
lose dialogues and faces.

I am afraid of being left defenseless,
afraid that the new deluge
will completely overflow
the old signs
and that my landscape
will turn into a hostile land
without relief.

Today I was able to find
an evening in Valparaíso:
a little petrified,
but that doesn't matter.
I recognize the outlines:
Mariluz's eyes,
her expression,
against the tinplate background
of a house
overlooking the bay.

# Self-Portrait

The eyes, badly captured.
Side view of a timid little girl,
curls disheveled,
teeth, uneven.
Tense cords running up my throat.
Cheeks shiny,
no features.
Torn apart.
All I have left are pieces.
My dresses from then are worn out.
I have new fingernails,
different skin.
Why does memory last?
There was a time of graph-paper landscapes
of people with eyes badly set,
noses badly set.
Tongues sticking out like thorns
from afflicted mouths.
Neither did I find myself.
I kept looking
in conversations with my associates,
in conference rooms,
in libraries.
Everyone, like me,
circling the hole.
I need a mirror.
Nothing covers the open pit.
Only fragments and the frame.
Sharp fragments that hurt me
reflecting an eye,
a lip,

an ear.
As if I didn't have a face,
as if something synthetic,
shifting,
oscillated in four dimensions
slipping sometimes into others
still unknown.
I have changed my shape
and my dance.
I am going to die one day
and I don't know my face
and I can't come back.

# Multiple Monologue

*In one sense, the archetypes are the universals
in man, the psychic potentialities latent in
mankind as a whole.*

—IRA PROGOFF

Mother:
At last I take pleasure from
your being here.
You were born at the moment,
at the precise instant,
meant for you.
It's autumn in the parks,
in the wind.
For you the roads,
so you may cross them.
There are deserts of sand.
Among all voices
you will have to hear your voice.

Lover:
Look at the fish leading the dance.
Look at it shivering with fright.
The pool is small,
but not for it,
for it finds itself alone and lost.
Come closer, love.
That was me
before I found you.
The world was very large to me.
Now your presence fills it
as your reflection fills this pool.

Warrior:
It's difficult to explain
the things that happen to a person.
Or to completely understand them.
That winter,
when starving wolves
surrounded me,
and I had nothing
but the stone in my hand
and my defenseless family
in a cave.

Old Man:
I don't want to talk about death.
We are climbing, climbing.
I hear water falling
and it frightens me.
The serpent changes its skin.
I hang from its gaze.
After the funeral
we learn a little.
While the wound pains
we remember.
It heals and I forget.

Artisan:
It isn't possible that we're peaceful.
I've seen faces in the streets.
What shall I do with my hands?
Here I am at the end
up on a ladder
that was given to me.
I haven't yet found the stone,
the one that I must set in place,
the one that others will step on,
those who come later.

Mother:
There are dark taverns
and there are waiting eyes.
Plazas with hostile faces
and dirty barrios
and men who clutch their coffers
with convulsed hands.
Small reality, my son's.
He fits in a basket.

Lover:
Let's rest a while.
Here, on the sand.
Let's talk about our son,
about the son who still
remains in the future.
Think,
how day after day
I will come home,
I will take off my shoes by the fire
and I will watch him play
while you
come and go from the kitchen.
Maybe that's why
we lovers
are conservatives.
There are no spurs that incite us
to perform great deeds.
Our world is placid
and everything that happens outside it
scarcely concerns us.
We look at it through the window.

Warrior:
You have to see what a wolf is.
Man is clumsy.
The wolf,
legs like springs
and slaver dripping from its fangs.
What did I do to kill them?
Or that other time
when without wanting to
I entered the dragon's cave.
I had only a lance.
It's difficult to explain
the things that happen to a person.

Old Man:
But really what is a scar?
Mine has already opened several times.
When I was frivolous
and tickled by love.
Everything was new then
and it shone
like sunlight on the sand.
My desires rose vertically.
When time began to
blanch my hair
and I returned from my odyssey,
and now, just recently.
They say
that the universe is nearly ours.
but I have seen fish
poisoning themselves with blood.
Every twenty years
women come out into the streets
with their prayers.

Artisan:
What shall I do with my eyes
if I don't do it right?
They will have no meaning,
or my arms either,
or my childhood.
Others were here before me.
The stone tells its story.
Force my way
from a dark tunnel
and come here to immolate myself.

Mother:
Sleep,
rest,
grow.
I will not be able to help you.
Like all of us
you will always be alone
when it is time to choose.

Lover:
I defend my world
and let him defend his.
I am as important as he.
I am the measure
against which his feats are judged.
Come closer, love.

Warrior:
Later in Warsaw
dying with thirst
in a ghetto,
arms folded across my chest,
enduring.

And suddenly,
something happens
and I knew I had to fight
and we fought
and we were magnificent.
What has always saved me?
Some say faith.
Others, destiny,
a miracle.
I keep going, not understanding.
It is difficult to explain
the things that happen to a person.

Old Man:
Every time it's bigger.
We are becoming powerful.
The collapse is bigger.
Young men are needed,
men who haven't seen
the serpent change its skin,
who do not have bones sodden
from the rains,
and who speak about death
with no sense of the tomb.

Artisan:
I didn't choose
to have been born.
Even less,
to serve as a martyr.
But it is my turn now,
and I must take my place,
harden myself,
be pulsing stone
that others will step on,
those who come later.

# My Neighborhood

It is as if suddenly
I had stepped on
a white-hot live wire.
As if a thousand needles were pricking my skin.

I am afraid of people
who have never felt an electric shock,
who have never fallen into a well of cold water.
I should feel pity for them,
but I am afraid of them.
They remind me of death.
I live in a neighborhood of the dead.
Flowers,
leaves,
wind,
struggle against them.
Death hangs like smoke
and covers my neighborhood.
Every day
I converse with the dead.
The dead with empty eyes
and indecisive gestures.

Sometimes they transmit it to me.
I have seen my friends die.
I have talked to them afterward.
I have gone to their houses
and have drunk tea with them.
But it's different now.
A patch of cloud
divides the blue sky.

The gull has dived
with its triumphant cry
toward the always sea of always
warm, newly born.
I have again been burned
by life
and I carry its lightning in my eyes.

# Epitaph for a Dog

*For Erik*

When a dog dies
it stays dead.
I'll take care of it,
you assured me;
as if it had to do with springs
and gears.
The word *death*
leaving its mark on you.
It has a cutting edge,
a sense of guilt
and of the end.

We'll take him to be buried.
There's a ditch out back
with sides of clay.
A gaping hole
where dogs end up.
You don't look at me the way you used to.
Your childish games
now tainted with death.
We've been left alone:
you,
me,
looking at each other from a distance
across the pit.

# Apprenticeship

I can't remember
what we said,
how it went.
My dresses were long.
I combed my hair in a bun.
It happened.
That was all,
when I was innocent.
There were presages:
a craving for streets,
for long walks,
for crushed dry leaves.
Sitting on my hill
I watched evening fall.
The countryside was shining:
purplish blue
dense blue.
It would have been difficult not to love
given that time,
that landscape
and my innocence.
I began to know myself.
I waited for my daughter with amazement.
I was growing with her.
I discovered my fingers,
I picked up trifles with my fingers
and I was happy.
Snapping wood frightened me,
I laughed at my fear,
registered voices
and gestures.

The rest,
could have been an accident.
But here,
before me,
my daughter.
Destiny was closing one door to me
and opening another.

Then came a time of concerts,
of balls,
of *señores* kissing my hand,
of matrons wearing tiaras
and cocktail smiles.
I began to distance myself.
It was a time of jealousy
and discord
and emptiness.
One evening when I returned
I barely caught up with him.
I called him at the top of my voice.

"Let's talk," I said.
"Who are you?"
The role of mother is honorable,
necessary besides.
And that of woman too,
and neighbor.
There is no empty time in my day.
All the spaces are filled
with broken fingernails,
with greengrocers,
with bills that must be paid.

I am wasting myself on all that,
I am leaving bits of myself
in every corner.

I discover myself
on the dining room table
as I am dusting,
in the children's uniforms,
on shirt collars.
I don't find myself for days.
I walk past the mirror
and my image isn't reflected.
I don't have time
to talk with myself.
Nor do I blame myself at times.
I live when I am rewarded
with sunsets
and my son's laughter.
I accept arguments,
sleeplessness,
disillusion.
I cannot tolerate indifference.
At times my husband
with the air of a wise man
says that life is hope.
I smile
and say yes to please him.
But here, just among us,
I have never believed it.
Life for me
is horror of the void.
When I was innocent I didn't yet know.
Later I understood,
I fought the void,
I fight against it every day.

Life is not hope,
it is more volatile,
more precise.
A something less than love,
a something more than the journey.

# The Search

If my torch goes out it will be dark.
Dark as it is behind my eyes.
My voyage with no return
and this tunnel, my tomb.
A tunnel like a mother's womb.
The same architecture.
Its climate of signals and penumbrae.
Through this labyrinth until I find it.
Through this womb where rivers are born.
I will never again fear the height of winter
or the fallen maxillary.
In sanctuaries of shadow
constructing castles with my seashells,
with dead butterflies and leaves.

Someone is watching me.

The dagger leaps from my fingers
and turns against me.
We look at each other, stark still.
My hand reflected.
The dress that envelops me.
The same forehead.
Suddenly me with my opium eyes.
I thought I would have the form of a serpent,
that I would be an insect.
Suddenly me.
Will I make a tomb from the tunnel?
Outside, the wind is waiting.

My disguises, my veils,
lie here, destroyed.
Will I be alone until I die?
Every morning I will know.

# Dialogue

I have to give you my news.
Despite the sun
I am going to take you
to a corner of shadow
where the world will reach us
in soft murmurs.
I want to transfix you with my eyes
and say:
"Look at me,
don't turn away.
I love you,
but there is something more,
something I have nourished in my vigil,
that I cleared of brambles and weeds.
It is green,
vertical.
All my 'I's' have learned it
but I have not been able to explain it to you.
There were bits of afternoons.
They are so banal
that it is painful to name them:
Hours of light
and poems
and waves on the beach.
Don't move.
The next step
is the most difficult,

it is to reach you,
to give you my news
with a gesture
before I speak.
If you understand,
the universe will emerge from us
renewed,
sanctified."
You smile.
Your eyes are focused on the void
over my shoulder,
on the unassailable wall of my convent.

# Solitary Confinement

Here there was a garden
with a tree,
six birds,
the sun.
Tense with life I waited for you
but you didn't come.
I wanted to safeguard the tree
and its leaves,
I built a wall
against the wind,
I was harsh
and I was tender.
You didn't come.
The birds
grew impatient.
I was afraid
and I stopped them.
I wanted to save everything for you.
You didn't come
and you didn't come.
The leaves fell
among dead birds.
The tree turned into
a table,
a chair.
Bricks
closed off the sky
and the magic was gone.
I don't wait anymore.
Even so
I miss you terribly.

Every morning
in my cell
I sit down to remember.
I do it out of habit,
because I do,
to see if the garden revives
that time and drought
consumed,
my eagerness to keep it for you.
I can at times almost
see your leaves,
hear your song,
feel your sun.

# Inner Minute

I am going to strip this minute bare,
divest it of its clothes.
I am going to strip it
as no one has ever done before,
as no one will ever do after me.
Because I am unique.
Who can take my place?
This minute,
the one I have invented,
is different from yours,
so different
it seems from another planet.
Who am I like?
You?
I don't know you.
I would like to exchange ideas.
Later, of course,
it must be later.
I have so much to do
inside myself.
I have barely removed
the first cloth
from the minute.

Who am I?
I am the dress
I saw this morning in the shopwindow.
I am the student
and daughter of the fisherman,
in the Saturday matinee,
they fight,

they make love,
and they walk arm in arm along the beach.
I am the heel
that must be repaired
and it reminds me with every step of
the fifteen pesos I need
to pay for the milk.
I am all these things.
Sometimes I ask myself
how much I am my desire
to act like a wife,
mother,
housewife
the one who haggles with the butcher,
keeps an eye on her garden,
makes no mistake
in the checkbook,
knows to fill the car
with gasoline,
oil,
water,
air.
Very little I think.

# ONE WAY
## (1965)

*Translated from the Spanish by*
*Margaret Sayers Peden*

## Pirouettes in a Room of Mirrors

It hasn't happened yet,
but I see myself
in the midst of locomotive smoke,
the voices,
the coming and going of passengers.
Or on a deserted dock.
Your handkerchief,
you,
my ship sailing away,
the mournful cry of my ship.
Little by little winter
has worn me down,
its black trees,
its muddy waters
licking the stones,
the fallen mist
over a horizon of wire
and chimneys.
An abyss at my side.
No one else sees it.
An abyss of voices,
of eyes,
of ghosts.
Hands keep on sprouting.
Eugenia's hand,
her tremor.
My daughter's hand,
her drawing.
All the hands asking me,
demanding of me,
and I can't.

All the hands like plagues,
fires,
cataclysms await me,
stripping me,
crushing me.
I carry your face mixed in
with orthopedic-shop windows,
traffic signs,
ads for aspirin.
I am water,
foam,
that cloud in the sky.
It hasn't happened yet,
and I already think of our love,
in the days,
in the hours of our love
as if the book had closed
forever.

# Though It Only Lasts an Instant

*To Bud*

Now,
while the obsidian river
reflects our image,
I want to speak to you of love,
of our love,
of the different threads
of its pattern,
of the love you can touch
that is a wound
and also soaring flight
and wakefulness.
Without it,
the green of these leaves
would have no meaning,
nor that streetlight
shining on the water,
nor the undulating image
of the church.
My love is the begging cup
where you tossed a coin—
it's the coin tinkling *I exist,*
the braid woven by our words,
the wine
and the sea from our table,
it's the misunderstandings,
the days we realize
we are no longer one,
that we are irremediably apart.
Yesterday,
from my exile,
I invented your arrival.

I broke through the ice,
startling the penguins,
scattering the stars
to await you.
I wanted to help you plant banners,
kneel beside you
to celebrate the miracle.
There I remained
with my flags.
Does my vertigo surprise you?
I'm talking about this:
the joyful stab
of knowing, *yes*,
that suddenly it's true,
that I am not alone,
that we are together beneath this tree
with my hand in yours,
that the river reflects us,
that now,
in this now,
in this instant,
though it only lasts an instant,
you are with me.

# The Grandfather

He looks at me,
from a daguerreotype
with an oval frame.
A fragile figure,
his hand resting
on the baroque back
of a chair,
the sunken throat
behind a high collar.
For me he was the trunk of the family tree,
my only grandfather.
He was born a grand *señor*.
His life,
a slow bankruptcy.
In the house of old walls
a meter thick,
sitting on the window bench
he would tell me about his aunt,
how she would roll
tobacco leaves
and laid her silver coins
to sun in the patio.
From the plane,
that is bringing me,
I imagine his expression.
I feel far away from him.
I picture the countryside,
walked at a man's pace,
the leaves,
the grass,

the dark volcanic earth,
the huts
with their *izote* fences.

He lived in Paris,
the Bois de Boulogne in a carriage,
concerts,
champagne,
a Salvadoran Don Juan
with a top hat
and a cane.
I am the fruit of his defeat,
the second harvest
of his graying years.
Before the tall desk,
without taking notice
of the advancing twilight,
he slowly recited Lamartine.
He did not see what was coming.
Bankers took
his estates.
The wine cellars,
the coffers
were emptied.
He continued absorbed
among his books,
musing over Voltaire
and Buffon
in his large library,
defenseless.
The sheets of linen were sold,
the silver service,
the children gave up
high school
and the grandmother died.
Now there will be a roof over the patio.

The new owner praises the desk.
It has several drawers
for accounting books.
I smile,
I say yes.
I run my hand
over the wood.
I look at the dust,
the white, century-old dust.
With a finger I draw
a doll,
a little girl with braids
and a short skirt.
I smile,
I say yes,
why not,
and of course.

# It's Growing Late, Doctor

He came from El Salvador on a mule,
he came from Estelí,
from Nicaragua,
from that blue country
with the smell of cattle and *tiste*.
He studied under streetlamps,
he won a gold medal.
But no.
I want to be more exact.
I see him carrying us on his back on the patio
playing the lion to frighten us,
looking into my eyes saying:
"For an old man
a child always
has a heart of glass."
I remember my choked wonder, my questions.
The whitewashed walls,
my thin legs that never rounded,
the arches,
the jasmine,
my mother's carriage,
the ring of keys at her belt.
Sometimes at night,
while the moon
lit the cats on the roof
and crickets shrilled,
he told us of Sandino,
of his men,
of long marches through jungle,
of the yanqui Marines
whistling down in their Helldivers

to break the column.
He told us of cesareans,
of discovering the crouched child.
On foggy days we climbed
the volcano,
mist licking our legs,
the branches with orchids and moss.
We climbed to the sun,
to the very peak,
once more to the sun of Central America.
I wanted to run,
I was the mother looking after a nest of birds.
I smoothed our tablecloth.
My brother, chanting,
skipped stones over the sulfur and emerald lake.
Your patriarchal air
frightened us.
You ruled the table like a feudal lord.
I want to tell you
about me, how I am.
I am still selfish.
I continue weaving
plots to win love.
It's growing late, Doctor.
We have both stayed
until dawn beside a sick child,
we grew bored among strangers,
we were ridiculous,
we stumbled and fell,
we had to accept that.
You left me riches:
Sandino, for example,
the Union of Central America,
the need to have a cesarean.
Exile hurts us.
At times, being parents annoys us.

I still think of myself first.
I am not your daughter now,
but your accomplice, your partner.
My defeats,
my struggles
have made the tears easy.
I think of you while
I think of myself,
of things that happen.

# Morning Thoughts

Today the light is milky.
Smells come fluttering to me.
The things I remember,
like an awkward colt
attacking my mother's lap.
Didn't you feel it that way?
I met you in a noisy
drawing room.
Talking about India,
about T. S. Eliot,
about Italian neorealism.
From my twenty years I was watching you,
from my solitude
and my desire.
Now faces emerge,
exhausted waitresses
hostile as they pick up
the menus,
shop clerks
who called me "honey."
In the middle of the asphalt
you offered me an oak.
It was only on loan,
An I.O.U.
With faint aromas,
with pleasant words,
we measured our solitude.
I'm bothered by birds that shriek,
your political ideas,
unevenly hung paintings.
We were two impermeable

loners.
With a stealthy determination
we made budgets
and made love.
I learned that laughing is comforting,
that the heat of your skin,
without words,
without sex,
hides the void for me.
I am a buoy,
a cork
rising
and falling,
a wing tempered by the wind,
a hoarse scream,
futile,
begging for tenderness.

# Documentary

Come, be my camera.
Let's photograph the ant heap,
the queen ant
extruding sacks of coffee,
my country.
It's the harvest.
Focus on the sleeping family
cluttering the ditch.
Now, among trees:
rapid,
dark-skinned fingers
stained with honey.
Shift to a long shot:
the file of ant men
trudging down the ravine
with sacks of coffee.
A contrast:
girls in colored skirts
laugh and chatter,
filling their baskets
with berries.
Focus down.
A close-up of the pregnant mother
dozing in the hammock.
Hard focus on the flies
spattering her face.
Cut.
The terrace of polished mosaics
protected from the sun.
Maids in white aprons
nourish the ladies

who play canasta,
celebrate invasions
and feel sorry for Cuba.
Izalco sleeps
beneath the volcano's eye.
A subterranean growl
makes the village tremble.
Trucks and oxcarts
laden with sacks
screech down the slopes.
Besides coffee
they plant angels
in my country.
A chorus of children
and women
with the small white coffin
move politely aside
as the harvest passes by.
The riverside women,
naked to the waist,
wash clothing.
The truck drivers
exchange jocular obscenities
for insults.
In Panchimalco,
waiting for the oxcart to pass by,
a peasant
with hands bound behind him
by the thumbs
and his escort of soldiers
blinks at the airplane:
a huge bee
bulging with coffee growers
and tourists.
The truck stops in the marketplace.

A panorama of iguanas,
chickens,
strips of meat,
wicker baskets,
piles of *nances,*
*nísperos,*
*naranjas,*
*zunzas,*
*zapotes,*
*quesos,*
*plátanos,*
*perros, pupusas, jocotes,*
acrid odors,
taffy candies,
urine puddles, tamarinds.
The virginal coffee
dances in the millhouse.
They strip her,
rape her,
lay her out on the patio
to doze in the sun.
The dark storage sheds
glimmer.
The golden coffee
sparkles with malaria,
blood,
illiteracy,
tuberculosis,
misery.
A truck roars
out of the warehouse.
It bellows uphill
drowning out the lesson:
*A* for alcoholism,
*B* for battalions,

*C* for corruption,
*D* for dictatorship,
*E* for exploitation,
*F* for the feudal power
of fourteen families
and et cetera, et cetera, et cetera.
My et cetera country,
my wounded country,
my child,
my tears,
my obsession.

# I.O.U.
## (1972)

*Translated from the Spanish by*
*Margaret Sayers Peden*

# The Almonds Are Blooming

The almonds are blooming
in Mallorca
and you are not here to see them.
From my balcony last night
I saw their phosphorescence.
I called your name,
I conjured up your ghost,
I outlined you with fallen petals
and a gust of air
swept you away.

# Dans le Metro

Indecipherable lights
and I leave them behind.
I saw you get off.
You looked for me an instant
wild-eyed.
"And your task for me,
what do I do?"
Everyone turns to look at me,
leaving me squelched in my seat.
Nothing to see out my window.
Cigarette butts on the floor,
Worn-out pumps,
*La vache qui rit.*
The smell of wine
and onion,
of life in the slow lane;
the dilatory bubbling of memories,
desires that leave their claw marks.
In that station of white walls
of white, antiseptic
walls.
Through the useless window
a reflection is watching me.
Now more real than my memory of you
and as useless.
You told me what to do,
you explained it to me:
your way of accepting my twists and turns
my countless amazements,
my questions.
Casual conversations

distract me,
overheard phrases,
faces with eyes like teeth
defending their space.
Through your open window
black birds are shrieking.
Rain,
black birds,
scraps of hoarse voices.
"Let go," you yelled,
"let go,"
looking for me with wild eyes.
I understood.
I thought I understood.
Through a grille of air
you escaped.

# Long-Distance Communication

*For Patricia*

No.
Don't insist that I come.
What can I do
for dying friends,
for Aunt Graciela
with her bubonic plague,
for Antonio
who will be executed
anyway?
Which ones demand my presence?
Yes, there are beautiful things in Santa Ana.
Of course.
And don't forget our *maquilishuat* tree,
or San Andrés in bloom
or the old trunk of the ceiba,
and the twenty-seven shades of green
in early morning.
The slaver of the beast
does not forgive.
What can they do with processions
and archiepiscopal and papal
benedictions?
It came
from the center of the volcano.
I remember it flowing down the flanks
and children crying
streams were annihilated;
trees fell
and all green was gone.
Today I will go by the pharmacy.
I will send boric acid

on the first plane.
Don't press me to come.
I have a sick little girl.
Excuses, of course, excuses.
I shouldn't have left.
I was afraid.
No one raised a voice
and all I heard were the grackles
and military motorcycles.
What were the mirrors for?
A peace conference
at the Versailles Inn?
I am nostalgic, yes:
the band in the central park
the way people say "Vaya con Dios"
all day long,
the puffy clouds
at noontime.
But the volcano roars
and my city is cast into mourning
with ashes
and lice
and heat
and mosquitoes
and bombing
and tidal waves.
It has stopped for the time.
They will be back laden with napalm
or nuclear megatons.
I can't bear the neighing
of the electronic heralds
or the tattoo of fire
or the soothing balm.
Ernesto wrote in a letter
that the protective ceiba had fallen
(and I hadn't gone to our rendezvous)

that angry blacks
barefoot guerrillas
students on strike
run through the plaza
that there are no palms
on the street of the palms
and those children from Biafra
have invaded the atria
of all the churches
and no one can understand their lingo
and gigantic medusas in the sea
prevent food from reaching them
and again that hand
drawing more sixes in the sky.

# The American Way of Death

*To Erik*

If you claw the mountain day and night
and lie in ambush behind the shrubs
(the backpack of failure growing heavier,
thirst opening cracks in your throat
and the fever for change
devouring you)
if you choose the guerrilla path,
be careful,
they'll kill you

If you combat your chaos
through peace,
nonviolence,
brotherly love,
long marches without guns,
with women and children
being spat at in the face,
be careful,
they'll kill you.

If your skin is dark
and you go barefoot
and your insides are gnawed by worms,
hunger,
malaria:
slowly they'll kill you.

If you are a black from Harlem
and they offer you football fields
paved with asphalt,

a television in the kitchen
and joints of marijuana:
little by little they'll kill you.

If you suffer from asthma,
if a dream exasperates you
—whether in Buenos Aires
or Atlanta—
that takes you from Montgomery
to Memphis
or across the Andes on foot,
be careful:
you'll become obsessed,
a sleepwalker
a poet.
If you are born in the ghetto
or shantytown
and your school is the gutter
or the street corner,
first of all you must eat,
then pay the rent
and in the time left over
sit on the curb
and watch the cars go by.
But one day the news reaches you,
the word spreads,
your neighbor tells you
because you can't read
or don't have a dime
to buy the newspaper
or the television is screwed up.
Whichever way,
you learn the news:
they've killed him,
yes,
they've killed another one.

# Suddenly

Suddenly
like the dark whistle of trains
your presence rises up in me.
A rooster's crowing is in the air.
I retrace our path
with your signs:
red stoplights
and green,
yellow silences
that I passed by long ago.
The air smells of Santa Ana,
of your overcoat flying in the corridor.
The rooster is still crowing
and you are not here.

# The Streams

*For Karen*

The streams are full
in Deyá
and the air transparent
and the sky and the sea
a purplish blue
and the stone walls
tinged with green.
No one speaks of death
today,
nevertheless it is here.
It took the house next door
by surprise
and wrapped in a blanket
the grandfather moans
and the dog barks
in the back patio.
"It's Francisca, *señora,*"
María tells me.
"They took her to the hospital yesterday."
All of us thought
it was the knot of veins
she had in her chest
but the doctor says
it was rabies.
"She carried it in her blood,"
he explains
as her daughter listens,
listens and learns.
You have to know how to behave
when faced by love

and scandal
and death.
It was like a worm
she carried in her blood.
She began to look sick
last night
and they took her to the clinic
and brought her home dead.
The little dog won't stop barking.

Francisca's daughters
go in and out,
they are pale
and they don't know what to do
and the wash that she put out yesterday
is still hanging
out there on the line
and no one comes to take it down.
Francisca's body
is already blue
and three women come
with a bride's dress
and the doctor has said
not to move her about
and two boys come
with buckets of lime
and the husband tells me:
the pain
and the asphyxia,
and he can't swallow.
And all the while the dog
keeps barking
in the back patio
and the clothes on the line
make futile gestures

and Francisca lies
there on her bed
and the old women dress her
in her bridal gown
and the wife of her lover comes in.
Francisca was beautiful
and she had a lover.
The wife comes in
with tightly pressed lips
and eyeglasses
and in her hands she's carrying
the wreath
she wore on her wedding day
and while the old women
step back with respect
she places it
on the brow of the dead woman,
on Francisca's
blue and icy brow.
The lover prowls around,
prowls,
he doesn't dare came in,
he doesn't dare howl
over the stiff legs
of the dead woman.
In Deyá
a person can't lose control.
He is the mailman
and everyone knows him.
If necessary he delivers every day
goes home at night
to confront those tightly pressed lips
the hard reflection of those eyeglasses,
and the absence of the wreath,
it is better to abandon the motorcycle
on a corner

and scout around
defying the looks
of the neighbors
going in to offer condolences
in the forbidden house
where Francisca
icy
and rigid
with the blue forehead
and the wreath
lies on her matrimonial bed.
"Francisca,"
says the husband
over the corpse
surrounded by neighbors.
"You left me alone, Francisca,
you caused a lot of talk
but you were a good woman."
The old women
hang cloth
in the way of curtains,
over the glass in the door.
"I loved you, Francisca,"
he keeps repeating
in a monotonous voice
while everyone looks at him
with respect
and the lover prowls
and the grandfather weeps at the hearth
and María bows her head
and the daughters look at faces
searching for an answer
and the little dog
that was barking on the back patio
now is howling
and the wash that

Francisca hung out yesterday
is still hanging
on the line
and no one comes to take it down.

# My Paradise in Mallorca

Each night
in my paradise in Mallorca
new phantoms surge up:
mournful, tangled moans,
the song of nightingales,
the wailing of a child,
the ancient eyes
of twenty-year-olds
that darken my sky.
It is summer
and the sea is warm
and smells of seaweed
and there is desire in the sockets
of your eyes
and another green swell
from the other sea
of my childhood
sweeps over my breast
one February 22
the day after Sandino died
and I didn't know
who Sandino was
until my father
explained
while we breasted the waves
and I was born.
It was then I was born.
Like Venus,
for the first time I saw light
through the foam.
Before, I was a plant,

a reckless tendril
that bent with the wind,
a pair of uncontaminated
empty eyes.
I came out of the sea
—my hand in my father's hand—
hating the Yankee minister
and Somoza
and that same night
I made a solemn pact
with Sandino
which I have not yet fulfilled
and that's why his phantom
pursues me
and the stench of repression
assails me
and it's not only Sandino,
I also made a pact
with the poor children of my country
which I also haven't fulfilled.
A child
dies of hunger
every five minutes
and there are crimes
and ghettos
and more crimes
committed in the name of order
in the name of law and order
and although the sea is warm
and I love you,
my paradise in Mallorca
is a closed room
that each night is peopled with phantoms.

# Elegy for Duncan

I don't know, Duncan,
whether you know
that the day after you died
the exodus began in Deyá.
First a pair
of young lovers,
then a girl
who ran through the streets
clawing her breast
and then that poet
with the somnambulist eyes
who wrote down
your last words.
With each one of them
some part of you left us.
We were being stripped of your voice
of your form
and little by little
those of us who stayed in Deyá
began wanting not to go out,
to avoid the café on the corner
where you sat to read.
It was difficult
to look in each other's eyes
with your death
wandering among us.
Without you,
without your closest friends,
only the uncomfortable
presence of your death
that clouded our words

and made us talk in hollow phrases.
Now things are more clear.
Your death has gone away
and you have come back
to rescue your image
and I laugh with you
when I talk
with the calves,
the way you taught me,
and they answer me
and once again
we all go to the café
and friends began to return
and we look each other in the eye
and hidden there
is your image
without the uncomfortable presence
of your death.

# Of Watermelons and Bridges

I am tired of your death.
I want to forget it now
and remember the rest.
The important thing is your passage,
the process,
the rings that link together
the chain,
that now tense, perfect
arch
I sometimes cross
when fear prods me
to misremember your face.
I want your life now.
Your death was astonishment,
a tearing and ripping,
a too-early good-bye.
Your life
not your death:
the bridge you built
hour after hour
(do you remember that hot day
when like two thieves we shared
the only watermelon?)
with small planks I helped you nail
and great gaps
I know nothing about.
Death is a fierce creature
a bloody knife blade
that cuts down everything around it,
a big absurd bird
that fouls my remembrance.

Your life and not your death
your face that evening
when you came home blazing with joy
and raising it high
announced to my mother
that now, yes,
now it's confirmed,
I saved
José Eduardo's leg.
I revive you in your yesterday
in our yesterday
and time doesn't exist
and you are watching over me
and your steps are my steps:
the ones we walked together
and others,
those that at the end,
while we were gathered around your bed,
you were walking alone.
Your every footfall resonated,
made us tremble.

And as you neared the end,
because you knew it was the end,
you turned your eyes
toward us
and disappeared into the mist.

# I Have Just Been Born

I have just been born
into my present
which has no beginning
no future
and I am held suspended
by your gaze
and my ears open
like a fruit
and your voice penetrates
and wakes me
and you go erasing spaces
with your hand
until you touch my body
which you invented
and I begin to remember
and the numbing bandages
of the night
began to fall in shreds
and it is a boat
filled with signs
the unreal reality
of our room
and you have been beside me
forever
since before the water
and the earth
long before the sun
broke into fragments
since we were one
and not halves.

# Santa Ana in the Dark

*To Maya*

Let there be darkness
declared Don Raimundo
the lights went out
Santa Ana grew dark.
My village was never bright
only forty-watt bulbs
swaying in little shacks,
lighting up some mending
some ironing,
school lessons.
It has been one hundred years
since the death of light
in Santa Ana.
Now the women light
their work with candles
and wake red-eyed.
The men have forgotten how to read
and at night they drink
take to the streets, bicker.
Only the children have reason
to be glad.
No one forces them to study.
Their script letters shrink
until no one can see them.
They won't learn their forty-watt history.

Each day when the sun drops,
Mama Clara, sitting by the sidewalk
recites Bible verses.
The neighbors ask her for Genesis
and they marvel at the power

of Don Raimundo
who had the gall to kill lights.
Don Raimundo is accustomed to command.
With the snap of his fingers
all is accomplished.
Last year alone,
said the foreman,
I told him we needed more trucks.
In less than an hour there were five.
We had to fill them in a hurry.
That is why I tell you
Don Raimundo is clever.
God rewards the clever
and punishes the rest of us
who go on stumbling.
Darkness was created
when my father died.
He was the village doctor
who brought his lamp from Estelí.
My grandfather
had carried it from Paris.
No one in Santa Ana
makes their own light.
Each time a lamp goes out
things grow murkier
and you look without seeing
and say yes with your head
and no one understands.
Ricardo lit matches
we could see our faces,
but the next day they closed down his school.
Jose Ángel
had a lantern.
Someone dropped it
and he picked it up
wanting to be like my father

bringing his light to our homes.
He died of tetanus.
Our house in Santa Ana crumbles,
writes my brother.
Little by little we abandon it,
one by one we leave it alone.
The garden once filled with birds is empty.
Poison finished Santa Ana's birds
and the flowers don't grow as before
in the garden of my house.
My mother tended the carnations,
she watered the grass
and nurtured the jasmine.
Now that she has gone
everything has died.

The dead eat their dead.
The wood decomposes.
The vultures, because they have vanished,
rot piles upon rot.
The faces in this album
smile at me, smelling of camphor.
Celia,
Isabel,
Margot.
They still dress up on Sundays
for High Mass in the cathedral.
It has been this way forty years.
They meet in the vestry
as they go out
they walk to the café near the park
for vanilla sweets and to gossip
among themselves.
Thank God they are virgins!
(All men are alike.)
At twelve each goes to her home

to be buried among
paper flowers and the silver Christ.
Sometimes in my dreams
I stumble over the eyes
of Don Santiago,
always the same eyes
that avoid me.
A straw hat protects
his bald head from the sun.
The same dull hello.
The feet that daily drag him
toward the kiosk,
from the kiosk to his house
with his daily paper.
He was clever once.
The whole village knows it.
He had a pharmacy,
sold everything cheap or on credit.
One day the village rose up.
Santiago himself against the police.
Don Raimundo ordered his pharmacy closed
and his wife died of yellow fever.
His sons fled.
Since then he has spoken to no one.
Each time I stumble over him
in my dreams I think I am
in the open country of death
and I wake chilled.
It didn't matter
when we were young.
Everything was green.
We grew up without knowing
of light in other places
and we marveled when someone
carried a lamp.
Sun and moon were enough;

the curtain of fireflies opening,
closing in the night.
The fat clouds.
The glow of the crater Izalco.
The fireflies.
And the morning star,
and Sirius
and the Seven Little Sisters
brighter in the darkness of Santa Ana
than anywhere else in the world.
All of this to tell you
I am desperate to go back.

# Cradle Song for Duncan James

Today is day of sun
of a stubborn miracle
of a rainbow.
You have opened a door
and we are walking round you
and we feel close by
and the sun is brilliant
it hurts your eyes
and you close them.
You have come to this planet
and you should know:
there are also rainy days,
long seasons
that darken the sun
days of cold wind
when you will open your eyes
and see gray clouds,
a dark sky
of omens,
piles of rubbish
in plastic bags
stinking, polluted
air
and fish die
and napalm falls from airplanes
and plants die
shrubs,
grass
and where there were meadows
with trees
and flowers

now there is
spreading leprosy.
I heard and saw you arrive
and you need to know:
it is not the best moment
to come to this planet.
The rain is unpleasant
but the sun, but the sun.
You do not yet understand:
a quarter of a century ago
we stole two particles
from the sun,
we threw them
on Hiroshima
and Nagasaki
and eyes turned into
enormous black holes
and disappeared
in fistfuls of smoke
and some survived
with cancer
skin
and bones
and children were born without hands
and without legs
brain damaged
blind
without a face.
We have progressed
since then:
we send astronauts
to the moon
and on the earth
we make caves
we bottle particles
of the sun

and carefully cultivate them
and when the astronauts
return
with maps of the moon
and the galaxies
our small suns
crouch
in their bottles
awaiting their turn
(twenty,
thirty,
maybe a hundred years),
they await the day
when mushroom explosions
will erupt
and dissolve the earth.
It is not the best moment
to come:
it is sad to wish for you only
days of rain
and omens,
but the sun is a spark
that incinerates you.
We celebrate it when it shines.
We go outside
and celebrate it.
Its heat
warms our bones,
it reaches us through
dense smoke
and the world turns green
and so do we
we have new vigor
and feel we are neighbors

and we look for other eyes
other hands
and we say
one to the other
that everything will turn out fine.
Better not to let ourselves be deceived.
Shut your eyes tight
and hear how it is raining
on other places:
right now
as I am talking to you
a viscous
and foul-smelling mud
is in the jungle shutting the eyes
of some youth,
a girl child is born to death
wrapped in flames
of napalm,
a barefoot
undernourished mother
walks
carrying her daughter's dead body
in her arms.
Better not to let ourselves be deceived.
Shut your eyes tight
against the sun.
On rainy days
they will open
and you will see gray clouds
and a melancholy sky
of omens.

# ROOTS
# (1973–1975)

*Translated from the Spanish by*
*Margaret Sayers Peden*

# It Is Closing This Door That I Fear

Here I am
definitively installed
in my present
with red gladiolus
a pitcher of wine
and the fresh memory
of your lips
it isn't fear of death
as you insist
for my death is far away
I don't glimpse its face
and it doesn't matter
if it reduces me to dust
perhaps the best would be
a long long
dream
in which you are disintegrating
it is closing this door
that I fear
closing this door
forever
making a hole in this wall
to suddenly find myself
on the other side
without a pitcher of wine
without your lips
without the red gladiolus.

# Autumn

You're in your autumn
you told me
and I felt myself tremble
a leaf of flame
that clings to its stem
that is resolute
that is a yellow eyelid
and a candle's light
a dance of life
and death
suspended brightness
in the eternal instant
of the present.

# I Am Root

More than polished stone
more than morning dusk
more than the dream of the tree
and those of flower and fruit
I am root
a winding, crawling root
without luster, without a future
blind to any vision
hardening the ground
as I work through it
testing the fallen bread
of misfortune
the opacity of wingless birds
the overshadowed dawn
and its leaden clouds
hours that pass without dark messages
an undulating, twining root
perhaps hanging up from the ground
that lightning, that stone
once on the beach moving among
weeds, alone among rubbish, searching
cinereous root, mortal root
diver of my darkest regions
obscure calligraphy
inheritance of gallows, of cabala
poison root
imprisoned by the time of a place
mirror of myself without water, thirsty
your blood tastes of the earth
your bark, summer
imprisoned, you don't look

for openings, you look for death
a quiet death, disguised
as days without omens
and as time without dates
and the gray willing faces of the hours
without birds where an instant
simply dissolves
the life I've yet to live
does not inspire me
in my lips there are crevices
and my face is stone
I do not allow a storm to enter
silently, I submerge myself
in a sea which no longer moves
the murmur ends
the appearances and disappearances
all dreams in which we can only
dream of ourselves
the remains of that daggered love
and the other, hidden love
the names of Eros and Thanatos
everything vanishes
your crystal song never reaches me
nor your wet touch
nor your lips
nor the teeth of your love

I gather my fragments and slip away,
I slither, I smell the sea
in which one day my memory will be
buried and I will not know pain
demands, or fear
and I will be then no more
than a calm spin in a tomb of water.

# Today I Was Born with the Dawn

Today I was born with the dawn
light came
dancing
into my room
and I felt happy
as I did as a child
and I danced with the light
and I heard the voice of the ivy
and the geranium
and I went dancing outside
and up the hill
with the light
and I sat down to watch it shine
on the grass
and with it I went down
to the edge of the sea
and I saw it shine
on the waves
and suddenly it was the sea
the murmur of the sea
in my ears
the smell of rotted seaweed
of rotted wood
of fishermen's nets
and I closed my eyes
and memories
came galloping in
and I lay on a rock
and with my eyes closed
and I couldn't bear
my life suddenly

marching by
my memories mingled
veered
opened
no one can bear
that much life
and I opened my eyelids
and there was light on the sea
and there was shadow
islands of light
and shadow
on the sky
and I began to rise up
and there was light
and shadow
on the colors
interwoven signs
on the ground
and I paused a moment
to decipher them
to draw more signs
to erase them
and the throng of memories
diminished
leaf by leaf
the memories fell
and I kept rising
lighter now
with the light
and shadow
flowing between my footsteps.

# I Am an Ordinary Skin

I am an ordinary skin
a skin stretched
above the dizzying edge
of an abyss
traveled
tattooed
by pin-sharp
memories—I remember
that they stick me
that they keep me focused
they're real
I finger them
I could if I wished
unpin them
begin at the center
the one at my navel
release the pattern
of its hooks
verify scars
burn from wounds
discover when they return
whether I will fall wrinkled
like bedraggled mourning crape
or whether alone I can
float above the void.

# And I Dreamt I Was a Tree

*To Carole*

And I dreamt I was a tree
with leafy branches
and the birds loved me
and the strangers
who sought my shade
loved me
and I loved my foliage,
the wind loved me
and so did the hawks
but one day
my leaves began
to weigh on me,
to obscure my afternoons
and filter out starlight.
All my sap
was thinned
for my lovely
dark-green drapery
and I heard my roots groan
and my trunk ached
and I began to disrobe
to shake myself
I had to free myself
of all that extravagance
of green leaves.
I began to shake myself
and the leaves fell.
Again more strongly
and along with the leaves that scarcely mattered
fell one I loved:
a brother

a friend
and all my most cherished illusions
fell to the ground
and my gods fell
and my friendly spirits
shriveled
and grew wrinkled
and turned yellow.
Scarcely any leaves
were left me:
four or five at most
maybe fewer
and I shook myself again
more furiously
and they didn't fall:
like steel propellers
they held fast.

# Beneath the Cold Skin of the Whale

*For Jean Marc*

Beneath the cold skin
of the whale
my pulse beats
and my ears open
am I rising?
sinking?
my eyes are open but I can't see
I perceive my form
by touch
feeling my way I look for
an opening
a way out
a flood of light
signaling to me.
I sniff the breeze
will there be sun on the water
or will it be moon?
the sea is panting
and I descend
run in clumsy
circles
I beat the air
with my fists
I call loudly
I don't want to
at last I am reconciled
I hear it raining out there
I hear the cruel screech
of the gull
I hear blue
and green

and purple
the sharp submarine rites
of the fish
that flash by in packs
of the octopuses
that fly.
The whale drags me
into its house
of shadow
am I alive?
have I died and don't know it?
I stick out my tongue
and laugh
I lash with my tongue
I moisten my lips
my lips taste of bile
from a sleepless
childhood
my ghosts
look at me
I am floating in the darkness
what will I be when I emerge?
I play myself a game of chess
what will the beach be like?
I will dance across the rooftops
of the houses
I will plunge deep into the woods
I will plant signs
on the wind
or maybe turn into
a seashell
and a child will pick me up
and in his room
listen to the sea.
Movement is simple
a leap

a single leap
the door will open
I am in transit
I sense myself in the dust
and in the leap
in the motionless vertigo
I sense myself.

# Root Mother

It was the insistent whistle
maybe the shiver
the scent of jasmine on the terrace
that turned to sulfur
in my lungs
and made me slip back
toward the past.
You led me to the patio
again I saw as then
the Seven Little Sheep
brighter
taller
more profound.
There was a new moon
and you pointed to it
"the silver ship"
that I found unbearable
when years later
I could see it only
as an ordinary silver-colored boat.
You opened windows for me
you introduced me to Humboldt
to Gustave Doré
and I can't quite remember
whether you said it
but in any case you thought it
(you have the benefit of
the wisdom of the serpent)
there is another world
beyond Santa Ana
and I discovered that world.

You showed me Paris
on postcards
and I knew that I had to live it
you had sentenced me
to live Paris.
As I was enjoying a sorbet
in La Florida
you told me
about your three divine poets
from that moment
I haven't been able to rest
I have spent my years
digging tunnels
getting dirt on my face
chewing spitting
the hard coal of poetry.
At times I look up
and your scales are gleaming
in the light of the moon
and I am blinded by
the emerald reflection
of the moon
in your opium eyes.
You are the anaconda
that is going to swallow me
the anaconda that ripples
its mottled scales
with its eyes fixed
on me
the old moon
in whose flames
I am beginning to be consumed.
I must understand you,
assimilate you,
turn you into an earthworm,
one by one separate

your segments
cut you into pieces, Mother,
and in each piece
make vertical sections.


**First Segment**

You were twelve
and you were a champion skater.
Something I could never do
I tried several times
and ended up with
battered knees.
I admired Sonja Henie
on the silver screen
she floated over the ice
of Rockefeller Center
and had your face
the same haughty carriage
your smile.
I saw you leap
give yourself airs in the arms
of your winged partner
but there was no ice
in Santa Ana
your skates had wheels
and squealed
across the hard paving stones
of the central park.
Maybe you didn't fly
the way I remember
but it's not important
your face was aflame
your black curls
floated in the air

you performed perilous pirouettes
you squatted down
with your arms around your knees
you rolled and rolled
and it was close to flying.
When did you lose
that joy?
When did you become
the cautious girl
who hung up her skates?


**Second Segment**

You were nineteen
and you spoke French
and played waltzes by Chopin.
In the afternoons
sitting on the bench
by your window
you read Sor Juana
Victor Hugo
and so no one would disturb you
Grandfather tiptoed
toward you
to close the door.
Sometimes you sat without reading
staring
hoping to envision
the white knight
of your dreams.
Suddenly Grandfather
lost everything
and you had to give up

that trip to Paris.
Later you fell in love
and your mother died
and a Gypsy
told your fortune
she saw you encircled
by a veil of tears.


## Third Segment

You were thirty-six
and had a grand piano
you almost never played.
Painters and poets
filled the house
you attracted them there
—lunar butterfly—
you perfumed the room
with your despotic fury
and silently
they fell in love
But one April day
your son died
and you lost interest in
your salon
you retreated into yourself
you read the theosophists
and it was then,
I see it clearly now,
that you gave up on yourself
that you withdrew.

## Fourth Segment

I was irritated by your jealousy
your rancor
your pursuing my father
beyond his death.
You became obsessive
(about your only nourishment
it was marmalade and bread)
you turned away from your books
your friends
you could not go out alone
(the streets faded in your memory)
or uncork a bottle
or light the gas in the kitchen.
You have acquired the gift
of becoming invisible
you are here
sitting among us
but no one sees you
a faint whistle
suddenly
a whistle
that's all
and I know that you're here
that again you lift
your head
with your gaze fixed
on me.


## Fifth Segment

Now your photo
on my desk
the last

the one my brother took.
Sitting in profile
on the terrace
with your resigned
focused gaze.
I make an effort to reach you
and can't even
get a hint.
Sitting there
in your chair:
transparent
distant
powerful.
You are not thinking about your children
or about your life today.
Tell me what you are looking at
you've learned something
that I don't know how to decipher
I used to accept you
as mother
and that was enough
as anaconda mother
the one I had one day
to leave behind.
Tell me what you are looking at
you have shed your skin
and now I cannot understand you.
Tell me what, Mother.
Now that you are alone
now that you are the aged moon
the dark moon
black
floating in space
I can never come near.

# I Would Rather Go Back to My Spiders

I remember you on my lips
on my skin
in your open eyes
next to mine filled with turbid water
where lights and shadows
and frontiers
and trees
and faces
sail about haphazardly.
Was that reality
or dream?
Clearer than my face
are my dreams
your eyes are empty
emptier and emptier
my eyes are two fogged-over
mirrors
yours the
eyes of a skull
through which I look at stars
and empty space
in my eyes there are islands
specters
strayed loves
and smiles
(I am looking for the one
I lost in my childhood)
and spiders weaving
their obsession
and cities with birds
and bridges.

There is only empty space
in yours
I would rather go back
to my specters
it is black in your eyes
there are no stars
I would rather go back to my spiders
your eyes are my death
it has seen me
I cannot go back
to my turbid waters.

# Dreams Know Not Where to Run

The abyss is phosphorescent
it dazzles me
it moves on
it is a sky in reverse
a trap
hell
a great well with transparent walls
where time circles around
biting its own tail
and dreams know not
where to run
and there are gusts of smoke
that reveal
that cover
and unnamable suns
and ossuaries
and you are below
with the secret
I observe you from above
crouched
you open your fist
and close it again
and your face is mocking
and it is mine.

# I SURVIVE
# (1978)

*Translated from the Spanish by*
*Margaret Sayers Peden*

# I Thought I Would Spend My Time

I thought I would spend my time
loving
and being loved
I am beginning to realize
that I spent it doing harm
while I, in turn,
was
being
                    done
harm
                              to.

# Frontiers

I was the cloud
and the rain
and the sea
and I want to be the twilight
and the city wall
and you.

# Everything Is Normal in Our Courtyard

Despite the sun
and the air
the doves
the inquisitor continues
to cultivate his roses
pulling out weeds
rocks
tangled roots
he turns over the earth
looking
breaking it up
looking again
not tamping it down
the *marquesa* has crocheted
forever
every time someone passes
her glasses slip off
slight shifts of voice
to indicate her rank
alone the man dances
he wants to break his shadow
into a thousand pieces
he the crucified
is getting old
no one listens any more
to his prophecies
the iconoclast clown
approaches him
and sticks a cigarette
in his mouth
puff maestro

puff
instead he spits it out
and the beggar
squats and picks it up
the clouds are resplendent
the scent of jasmine rises
up the walls
the jailer paces
in white
looking for his friend
the priest
the executioner has arrived
and it's time
check
the general announces
the other jumps
lands on the board
moves his bishop
checkmate
the general fires
and his opponent
falls face down
I leave the inquisitor
squashing worms
everything is normal
in our courtyard
with fists
feet
saliva
two men are fighting
one wants
the other to tell him
who knows what
he doesn't know
or the other one either
the psychiatrist comes toward me

I concentrate on not calling him
Papá God
who's right?
I ask
I point
I wait
he smiles
and asks:
How are those poems going?

# Dream

*For Cristina, for Lil*

I dreamt
I was a wing
I was waked
by a tug
from my roots.

# I Bring Flowers Do'tor

I bring flowers, Do'tor.
In eleven years
memory has faded a little
and grass is growing on your grave.
A swarm of children
assaults us
they assure us, yelling
that for only two *reales*
we will find it clean
tomorrow.
My brother is impatient
they've never carried through
children keep coming
they're all around us
none looks like he'd finish
but maybe,
noisy, avid
children
defying the silence
the desolation of the cemetery
dark-skinned children with big eyes
who lift up their faces
and offer to look after death
for two *reales*.
I bring roses,
gladiolus,
daisies,
a branch of pine
so you can breathe in the scent of Nicaragua
of "Las Nubes"
following your wishes

sown only with pines.
It was your "Las Nubes" dream
to return some day
to that clean air
to the ravines
to the wild horses
to the cattle
to your earthly paradise.
You paid off the mortgage
three times you paid it
from exile
but were never able to return.

"You know?" my brother says
"When at last I could go
I found no pines
or streams
or cattle.
There were dry streams
thistles clinging to my clothing
and a fine, stubborn
dust
that turned our hair white."
The washerwomen are still there
doing the wash.
The *amate*
the ceiba
the palms
along this same route
on a different evening in May
happiness in your eyes
your smile
two children at the edge of the road
who've seen you and are jumping
and waving their arms.
"Do'tor, Do'tor," they shouted

you wave to them from the car
and leave them enveloped
in clouds of dust.
Candelaria
Chalchuapa
the flowering San Andrés
the narrow, insistent curve
that leads us to the *finca*
the wood portico
the cart in the courtyard
your voice announcing your visit:
"Niña Chon, Niña Chon"
an uproar of dogs
running out to meet us
the hugs
the laughter
whispers
"Back in a second"
Niña Chon brings me a glass of *atol*
a roasted ear of corn
fresh cottage cheese
and Antonio comes leading a black colt
and you behind
with your excitement
"It's for you" you tell me
"for you to ride"
my happiness
my fear
you help me up
you lead the colt
by the bridle
the uproar of dogs
other children watching
and smiling

the walk through coconut palms
and flame trees
Niña Chon denying that it was late
have more *atol*
more cottage cheese
the good-byes
the thanks
my feverish chatter
the same children with the big eyes
waiting for us to come back
"Do'tor, Do'tor," they shouted
you stop the car
"How on earth?" you say
"you've been waiting a long time."
"Going on four hours"
they laugh in chorus
and offer you a chicken
bees' honey
and a branch of mangoes
and star apples.

"He never knew
and just as well
they turned his paradise
into a hell."

You determined your climate
planted pines all around you
you gave away colts
you battled other people's deaths
you helped children be born.
We've left behind
your grass-covered tomb
withered memory
children with the look of not carrying through
let's also forget

the dry streambeds
the thistles
the dust
let's forget
the nephew who made fun
of your candor.
Saddle up two horses
right now
and take me to your meadow in the clouds.

# Love

*For Bud*

All the ones I love
are in you
and you
in everything I love.

# For Long Years

*To San Avilés*

For long years
I buried your voice
your voice was dense
and restrained me
I thought that you were dead
that I had buried you
I didn't hear your heartbeat
I didn't feel your fingers
pressing my temples
suddenly one night
you sprang up in my dreams
and I knew that it was you
you opened a way through the shadow
with a leap
you became a part of the day
I recognized your way of walking
like a guilty Gypsy
who predicts disasters
and later dances
on the ruins
I remembered you years ago
on the rocking horse
wanting to beat life
in the flanks.

# Sorrow

*To Roque Dalton*

## I

Voices that rise and are gone
*cuando sepas que he muerto*
*no pronuncies mi nombre*
(when you learn I have died
do not utter my name)
the dark shapes of friends
crying out
that break the fog an instant
a hand with no fingers
strumming a guitar
a single desperate sound
that lifts and escapes
I grope and it supports me
as it recedes.
Is that you, Víctor Jara?
These shadows of faces
that no longer exist
a broken word
small phrases so scattered
I can barely catch them:
*listos para la muerte*
*listos para vencer*
(prepared for death
prepared to conquer)
an echo reaches me, cut short
*Verde, que te quiero verde*
(Green, how I love you green)
It is a wave
a star

a transparency
*Puedo escribir los versos más tristes esta noche*
(Tonight I can write the saddest verses)


## II

Sun drenches the road
it isn't difficult to name
the trees, the streets, the church tower
the dry riverbed but there is light fog
and it veils the faces that were clear
the faces once clear grow hazy
when I want to know how to reach
the hidden tomb of the poet
I ask at a hotel, in a café
the alarmed expressions, the words
and the faces vanish
I do not understand
vague gestures and directions
*El crimen fue en Granada*
*en su Granada*
(The crime was in Granada
in his Granada)
everyone knows that
but no one is capable
of the precise detail
of saying for example
they flung his body down
at the foot of that olive tree
beside the young body
of a schoolteacher in glasses
I open the map
I set off down the dusty road
I pick some flowers
and shake the dust from them

another village ahead, another
no one knows here either
only an old official, his face
cracked with bitterness the same
rutted grooves as in the road
he answers me arrogant
our enemy the poet
he mutters that faggot
he walks off
*Verde, que te quiero verde*
(Green, how I love you green)
a fine stubborn dust
covers the olive trees there
is no tombstone
there are no clues
I open the map again
it must be close
I skirt the ravine
the one that swallowed the bodies
below me the house roof
that desolate room, your last
rung, intangible, real
a hundred meters ahead, La Fuente Grande
they didn't give you a grave marker
they did you the honor of tearing up
the twisted, the stubborn olive trees
*cuántos siglos de aceituna*
how many centuries of olives
*los pies y las manos presos*
the feet and the hands prisoners
*sol a sol y luna a luna*
sun to sun and moon to moon
*pesan sobre vuestros huesos*
weigh over your bones
they left only one tree, an olive
not even a stone reading

here lies the poet
but someone left a tree, an olive
someone knew and left it standing

# III

This mark on our foreheads
betrays us, the obstinate gleam
in our eyes of hunted animals
of vigilance, of calloused tears
we sense one another in the metro
we seek each other's glance then turn away
we walk aimlessly in cold streets
we avoid cafés
a smell of *guayabo* assaults in
the indifference of the world
the evening *mate*
the quick smell of bubbling stew
our country has fallen apart
it has gone bad
we roll in its filth
people avoid us
I don't know if it is our sweat
or the rotten taint of our land
a foul breath surrounds us
fumes that stink of helplessness
of stagnant dreams
of not having even small change
it forces us to tuck our heads
under the greasy collars of our coats
and keep walking, searching out comrades
*al mundo nada le importa*
*yira, yira*
(nothing matters to the world
it turns, turns)

we know one another by our grimace
by our damp eyes
we walk unhurried
we drift in search of a place
where we can wash ourselves
of the offensive odor of shame
we flee to the public baths
where all exiles congregate
and no one has even small change
the fungi pullulate
the cracks between our toes swell with fungi
but that does not matter
we must scrub off the stench of exile
we are stray dogs
it is better to have itching fungi
leaving our feet bloody
leaving a shriek within us
*me moriré en París con aguacero*
*un día del cual tengo ya el recuerdo*
(I will die in Paris with a heavy rain shower
on a day of which I already have the memory)


IV

Stubborn
confused
the news comes to me
truncated facts
cold, contradictory sentences
that pursue me
that is how your death arrived, Roque Dalton
the implacable news of your death
in the smudged headlines
your death in the bloodless voice of the radio
it arrived without precision

in broken images
you were a tower
a beacon slicing through fog
it is dangerous, Roque
to go about proclaiming Che
Jesus and Sandino
to ignore the real boss
to open your eyes
to feel that your own memory
opens wounds, each wound
a small flame rising
the echoes are still coming back
the false accusations
I'll never know who killed you
but you are dead, Roque Dalton,
and they wrap your death in fog.


V


We flee to the museums
they are nearly as cheap as public baths
we wander through salons
we sink into leather sofas
and sit for hours pretending to study
a Corot, a Cézanne
if the guard comes near us
we exchange enthusiasms
and stay longer
I close my eyes
the olive trees loom over me
the slaves
I see the outlines of night
dawn, day and midday
I take refuge in the arms of Mother Culture
and rest my infested feet in museums

again the slaves loom before me
trying to escape the stones that imprison them
I force myself to remember the Pietà
the Christ with one foot
the infant Christ
the slaves loom up
the olives
their twisted torsos haunt me

I return to the street to wander
their eyeless faces
their maimed desires
*andaluces de Jaén*
(Andalusians of Jaén)
*aceituneros altivos*
(haughty olive workers)
*decidme en el alma ¿quién*
(tell me in spirit who)
*quién levantó los olivos?*
(who raised up the olives?)


## VI

Only my footsteps on the walk
from a dark tavern
echoes of tangos, *milongas*
odors of sour wine and smoke
I hurry to the corner
the blinking neon
a voice detains me
a question
a face lights up
and is blue
it turns red
scarlet

I search for matches in my bag
a white mask
it observes me
it turns violet
it is your assassin, Roque
I light the face
it is only a boy still beardless
he smiles at me
the light is blue again
he moves off
it is your assassin
it is he
I don't dare
I let him pass
I am ashamed


## VII

Who raised the bars?
a gray light filters from outside
there is no sun
there are no birds, no foliage
they have sliced away the sky
I touch my stiff skin
I listen to my own panting
as from a distance
I need to remain myself
to leave the fog
throw off the terror
with a chip of coal I begin to write:
my loneliness, my—
the voices begin coming toward me
this backdrop of cries
punctuated by a scream
a sudden, a terrified silence

they start up again more loudly
shut up! the turnkey shouts
clanking his keys on the bars
no one listens to it
the voices of all
mingling in a solemn
a stubborn chorus that rises
swells, overflows
from my solitude I raise my voice
I ask and the answer is clear:
I am Georgina
I am Nelson
I am Raúl
again the tortured one
his howl and silence
I stretch out on my cot
with my eyes open
and not so much as a fissure of light
the screams are cut
I begin counting the names
my rosary of names

I think about the other
the next one who will sleep here
on my cot and listen
to the groaning hinges
and shit right here in this open pipe
hunched beneath his quota of terror
I return to my rosary
I am not alone
they are here
the transient guests
only a tissue of time
a tissue separates us
there is wine
there are guitars, tobacco

there are Víctor and Violeta
the shepherd poet
I leap from my cot
and stumble into Roque
I raise my finger to my lips
the laughter dies, the guitars, the eyes
I scratch on the wall:
they are more alone than we are.


## And the Eighth

Again, the scream
is it mine, is it coming from me?
From you, is it yours?
Gravely Melpómene
studies me
I pass before her eyes
from the turquoise heart
of a mosaic
her resplendence follows me
the bars do exist
they surround us
the cot also exists
with its hard sides
the river poem
that sustains us all
and is as substantial
as the cot
the poem that we are all writing
with tears,
with fingernails
and coal
the fiesta is over
the cigarette butts on the floor
the glasses are in shards

and we remain alone without guitars
without voices to sing
and the question rises, the challenge
tell me, in spirit, who
who raised up this prison's bars?

# Time

*For Julio*

I walked around
my past
my future
and suddenly
there was light from
my present.

# Little Cambray Tamales

*(makes five million little tamales)*

*For Eduardo and Helena, who asked me for a Salvadoran recipe*

Two pounds of mestizo cornmeal
half a pound of loin of *gachupín*
cooked and finely chopped
a box of pious raisins
two tablespoons of Malinche milk
one cup of enraged water
stir-fry some conquistador helmets
three Jesuit onions
a small bag of multinational gold
two dragon's teeth
one presidential carrot
two tablespoons of pimps
lard of Panchimalco Indians
two ministerial tomatoes
a half cup of television sugar
two drops of volcanic lava
seven leaves of *pito*
(don't be dirty minded, it's a soporific)
put everything to boil
over a slow fire
for five hundred years
and you'll see how tasty it is.

# At Night

At night
in dreams
more than one dead friend
revives
when I wake
I wonder
if they have also
dreamt of me.

# Evasion

*For Otto René Castillo*

We were talking about Shiva
about birds
about Barthes
you innocently plopped down
in the middle of us
and we kept talking
suddenly
during a pause
you interrupted the crochet
of our sentences
you threw open the window
and pointed out Claudio
lying quiet in his blood
there was silence
a halt
you closed the shutters
and Graciela
picking up her needles again,
announced:
I have to take out a whole row
I dropped stitches.

# I Am a Mirror

Water gleams
on my skin
and I don't feel it
water streams
down my back
I don't feel it
I rub myself with the towel
I pinch myself on an arm
I don't feel it
terrified I look at myself in the mirror
she pinches herself too
I begin to get dressed
stumbling about
from the corners burst
lightning flashes of screams
bulging eyes
scurrying rats
teeth
I still don't feel anything
I get lost in the streets:
children with dirty faces
asking me for coins
girl prostitutes
not yet fifteen
everything in the streets is an open sore
tanks rolling toward me
raised bayonets
bodies falling
weeping
at last I feel my arm
I'm no longer a ghost

it hurts
therefore I exist
again I look at the scene:
boys running
bleeding profusely
women with panic
on their faces
this time it hurts less
I pinch myself again and now I feel nothing
I simply reflect
what is happening around me
the tanks
aren't tanks
and the screams
aren't screams
I am a flat mirror
that nothing penetrates
my surface
is hard
is gleaming
is polished
I turned into a mirror
and have no flesh
though I do have
a vague memory
of pain.

# We Were Three

*To Paco and Rodolfo*

It was winter,
there was snow,
it was night,
this is a green day
of doves and sun
of ashes and cries.
The wind pushes me
across the bridge
over the cracked earth
through a dry streambed
strewn with cans.
Death comes to life
here in Deyá,
the *torrente*
the stone bridge.
My dead wait
at every corner,
the innocent grillwork of balconies
the filmed mirror of my dead.
They smile from the distance
and wave to me,
they leave the cemetery,
a wall of the dead.
My flesh emits light
and they come to my door
waving their arms.
The bridge was stone,
it was night,
our arms circled each other,
we swayed to our songs,
our breath rose from our mouths

in small, crystalline clouds,
it was winter,
there was snow,
we were three.
Today the earth is dry
and resounds like a drum,
my arms fall to my sides,
I am alone.
My dead stand watch
and send signals to me,
they assail me
in the radio and paper.
The wall of my dead
rises and reaches from Aconcagua to Izalco.
The bridge was stone,
it was night,
no one can say
how they died.
Their persecuted voices are one voice
dying by torture in prison.
My dead arise, they rage.
The streets are empty
but my dead wink at me.
I am a cemetery,
I have no country
and they are too many to bury.

# Flowers from the Volcano

*To Roberto and Ana María*

Fourteen volcanoes rise
in my remembered country
in my mythical country.
Fourteen volcanoes of foliage and stone
where strange clouds hold back
the screech of a homeless bird.
Who said that my country was green?
It is more red, more gray, more violent:
Izalco roars, taking more lives.
Eternal Chacmol collects blood,
the gray orphans
the volcano spitting bright lava
and the dead *guerrillero*
and the thousand betrayed faces,
the children who are watching
so they can tell of it.
Not one kingdom was left us.
One by one they fell
through all the Americas.
Steel rang in palaces,
in the streets,
in the forests
and the centaurs sacked the temple.
Gold disappeared and continues
to disappear on yanqui ships,
the golden coffee mixed with blood.
The priest flees screaming
in the middle of the night
he calls his followers
and they open the *guerrillero*'s chest
so as to offer the Chac

his smoking heart.
In Izalco no one believes
that Tlaloc is dead
despite television,
refrigerators,
Toyotas.
The cycle is closing,
strange the volcano's silence
since it last drew breath.
Central America trembled,
Managua collapsed.
In Guatemala the earth sank
Hurricane Fifi flattened Honduras.
They say the yanquis turned it away,
that it was moving toward Florida
and they forced it back.
The golden coffee is unloaded
in New York where
they roast it, grind it
can it and give it a price.
*Siete de junio*
*noche fatal*
*bailando el tango*
*la capital.*
From the shadowed terraces
San Salvador's volcano rises.
Two-story mansions
protected by walls
four meters high
march up its flanks
each with railings and gardens,
roses from England
and dwarf araucarias,
Uruguayan pines.
Farther up, in the crater
within the crater's walls

live peasant families
who cultivate flowers
their children can sell.
The cycle is closing,
Cuscatlán flowers
thrive in volcanic ash,
they grow strong, tall, brilliant.
The volcano's children
flow down like lava
with their bouquets of flowers,
like roots they meander
like rivers the cycle is closing.
The owners of two-story houses
protected from thieves by walls
peer from their balconies
and they see the red waves descending
and they drown their fears in whiskey,
they are only children in rags
with flowers from the volcano,
with *jacintos* and *pascuas* and *mulatas*
but the wave is swelling,
today's Chacmol still wants blood,
the cycle is closing,
Tlaloc is not dead.

# I Survive

I survive.
Wildly happy
I
  sur
         vi
ve.

# LUISA IN REALITYLAND
# (1983)

*Translated from the Spanish by*
*Darwin J. Flakoll*

# I Like Strokin' Leaves

More than books
magazines
and newspapers,
more than moving lips
that repeat the books,
the magazines,
the disasters,
I like stroking leaves
covering my face with leaves
and feeling their freshness
seeing the world
through their sifted light
through their greens
and listening to my silence
that ripens
and trembles on my lips
and bursts on my tongue
and listening to the earth
the breathes
and the earth is my body
and I am the body
of the earth
Claribel.

# Rainy Day

Never again this rain
nor that stain of light
on the mountain crag
nor the border
of that cloud
nor your fleeting immobile
smile
never again this instant
that already says good-bye
through your eyes.

# Disillusionment

I machine-gunned tourists
for the liberation
of Palestine.
I massacred Catholics
for the independence of Ireland.
I poisoned aborigines
in the Amazon jungles
to open the way
for urbanization
and progress.
I assassinated Sandino
Jesus
and Martí.
I exterminated My-Lai
in the name of democracy.
Nothing has done any good:
despite all my efforts
the world goes on just the same.

# My City

*The city will always pursue you.*

—C. P. CAVAFY

I dream that my city
was following me
I heard the internal music
of its insects
its foliage
its rock-strewn river
its odor obsessed me
its vaporous aromas
and sour sweatiness
and I wanted to flee from my city
from its muted groans
and rancid odors
and it followed me
with its row of faces
and streets
and its veiled laughter
and I turned to reprimand it
and it turned invisible
with no lights
or shadows
and its absence pained me
and nostalgia flowered in my dreams:
I retraced childhood paths
dreamt of friends I lost
of the trees
and the leaves I lost
of the town-hall band
of the *chiltota* nests
of my little white dress

and the bell calling me to Mass.
In a corner of the park
I awoke.

# Luisa's Paintings

Luisa always wanted to be a painter, but she had no talent. For her, painting was magic. She frequented museums and went to all the exhibits she could, because she was certain that in one of the pictures she would discover the secret: suddenly, right there in the center of the painting a door would open to let her into that other reality, which until now she had only conjectured.

Luisa imagined pictures that she was never able to transfer to the canvas, but one night she began to paint in her dreams. At the outset she used huge canvases of two by three meters with horizontal swatches of red shading into orange, or of violets that faded into white. Sometimes it took her several nights to finish a painting. She would think about it during the day, seeking solutions, and she would go to bed as early as possible in order to get back to work.

She spent a long time—more than a year—painting. The pictures grew smaller but were much more detailed. She painted artichokes; cabbages with eyes, noses, or ears lurking in the leaves; trains filled with people that climbed and swooped down roller-coaster mountains; plazas filled with empty chairs; black-frocked pastors preaching to starving dogs and two-legged cows.

Luisa began to think of organizing an exhibit. She had at least seventy canvases. The problem was finding a gallery. She would invite a group of her friends from that side to the opening: those she kept meeting in that other dimension.

One night she suddenly stopped painting. At first she gave the matter no importance; she must simply be tired and in need of a vacation. The terrible thing was that she had stopped painting when she was half-finished with a picture that disturbed her a great deal. She had gone back to swatches of colors. This one was a large canvas in different shades of gray with a line of red dots crossing it. The line went off the canvas on one side, and Luisa spent many days wondering how to finish it. She didn't know what the red dots signified. They didn't really fit into the painting and she wanted to eliminate them; the line of red dots that began dripping and running just before they went off the canvas.

A month went by, then two months. Luisa traveled to Nicaragua and began to work on something else, leaving behind that unfinished painting and the others—more than seventy of them—all stacked together.

# I Also Like That Love

*To Sara Jennifer*

I also like that love
that finds the door slammed shut
the one that enters through the window
pirouetting on a tightrope.

# Don't Think of Tomorrow

Don't think of tomorrow
or make me promises
you won't be the same
nor will I be present.
Let's live together the crest of this love
with no deceits
no fears
transparent.

# Roque's *Via Crucis*

"You can see death reflected in that boy's face," Aurora told Luisa, referring to Roque Dalton. "Nonsense!" Luisa exclaimed. "He has as many lives as a cat. He's always escaping death by the skin of his teeth. The first time he was saved by an earthquake. He was in the prison of Cojutepeque when an earthquake brought down a wall and he was able to wriggle out. The second time, he was only two days away from a firing squad when a coup d'état overthrew Lemus, who was the dictator at that moment."

Roque and Luisa never knew each other personally, but they corresponded between Prague and Paris and delighted in writing each other about Salvadoran *pupusas,* rooster in *chicha,* bread with *chumpe,* and all the other exquisite flavors and aromas that were unavailable to them in Europe.

Once Luisa traveled to Cuba, where Roque was awaiting her in the airport with a bunch of flowers, but her plane was delayed two days, and he had to travel to the interior of the island. From there he would send her notes, which were invariably delivered at lunchtime.

They never so much as embraced each other, but a mutual friend assured her that according to Roque, Luisa taught him to dance the rumba.

Years later, that same friend called Luisa to announce Roque's death. The news was confused, imprecise and nobody yet knew who had assassinated him.

Luisa was deeply touched, and that same evening, to feel a bit closer to him, she had the urge to read aloud some of this poems. She opened his book at random, and the first verses her eyes encountered were:

"When you learn I have died,
do not utter my name."

# Farabundo Martí

"Didn't Farabundo Martí enter this house about twenty minutes ago?" Colonel Salinas asked Luisa's father.

"No," he replied. "I've known Farabundo ever since we were at the university together. The only person who has knocked on the door in the past half hour was a beggar."

"Precisely. We have information that he has disguised himself as a beggar."

"Don't worry, Colonel" Luisa's father laughed, "I'd have recognized him."

"I'll take your word, Doctor, that you are telling me the truth," the colonel said as he went out the door.

Farabundo, in fact, was hiding in her father's clinic. General Martínez, who was defense minister at the time, had issued an order for his arrest.

Luisa's father went out to make his routine visit to his patients so as not to attract the attention of the guards across the street. The only one with whom he shared the secret was Luisa's mother, who took some sweet rolls and coffee to the fugitive and remained conversing with him for a while. About six in afternoon, Luisa's father returned home and sat down to read the newspaper as usual, so as not to arouse suspicions among the servants. Half an hour later, he slipped Farabundo into the garage, helped him into the trunk, and drove him to the Guatemalan border.

# The Volcanoes

Izalco no longer weeps
the volcanoes don't weep
no incandescent lava
flows down from their craters
waves of green
so sweeping up their flanks
beneath the greens
the *muchachos*.
Herds of Tlacoc
are the volcanoes
green bulls
who graze
on the igneous rock:
Chinchontepec
Guazapa
San Miguel
Their humps thrust up
and their skin undulates
shudders.
It's time for grazing
for storing up wrath
each pore of their skins
is a treasure trove
each pore shelters
a family
the fourteen volcanoes
belong to the people
not to the Fourteen Families
to the people
they nourish their *muchachos*
conceal them

speak to them of their future
of the tangible dream
of the fiery eye
that allows no sleep
that unites all of them
holding them in suspense
whirling about them
and in the middle
of night revives their dead
with torches of light
in their hands.

## Eunice Avilés

One time Luisa said she was an artist named Eunice Avilés, but she didn't mean to deceive. There was a retrospective exhibit of Matisse in the Paris Museum of Modern Art, and since she loved Matisse's work, she decided to spend the day there. At lunchtime, after having seen dozens of paintings, she went to the cafeteria and sat down—her feet were killing her—at the only vacant table. A few minutes later, a young man who looked to be American came up and asked if he could share the table with her.

He was, in fact, a gringo and a painter. He was enthused with the exhibit, and they began talking and exchanging opinions animatedly. After lunch they returned to the exhibit together, and Luisa suddenly found herself speaking with great self-assurance—a most unusual thing with her—about Matisse's work. She spoke with such authority that she couldn't assume the responsibility for her work.

"Are you an art professor?" the boy asked. "A painter," Luisa fibbed without faltering.

"Why didn't you say so before? My name is Michael Stone."

"Eunice Avilés," she replied, startled at this second unnecessary lie.

"I'd love to see your painting," Michael said enthusiastically. "Your observations and comments have fascinated me, and I'm sure I could learn a great deal from your work."

"I don't live here," Luisa said defensively. "I'm just passing through."

"Where do you live?" he asked.

"In Mykonos, in an old mill," Luisa heard herself say.

"Greece is on my itinerary, so I'll come and see you."

They continued looking at pictures and chatting animatedly. When the museum closed they went to a café near the Trocadero to have coffee.

"This has been one of the most pleasant days of my trip," Michael said, pulling out a small agenda. "Would you give me your address?"

"I have no address," Luisa laughed. "When you get to Mykonos, just ask for Eunice Avilés. It's a small island, and everybody knows my mill."

They parted with pecks on the cheek, and when Luisa had walked a few steps toward the Metro, Michael called to her: "See you soon."

Luisa started home with a preoccupied air and decided not to say a word to Bud, because he didn't like lies.

"Good grief! Why did I do that?" she asked herself as she boarded the metro. He's probably really going to Mykonos now. What got into me, anyway? Oh well, it will be worth it. Maybe something nice will happen to him on the island, and if it hadn't been for my absurd fibs he would never have gone. Besides, who knows? He may find the Gypsy waiting for him when he arrives.

# Salarrué

"I hate to see him when he's wandering around on the astral planet," Celie said. "It's almost as if he were dead. His body turns stiff and cold. The only thing that makes me feel easier is that he keeps on breathing, but just barely."

Salarrué, besides being a great story writer and excellent painter, also knew how to bilocate and see people's auras. He was always repeating to Luisa's mother that she had a beautiful aura.

Luisa was a close friend of his daughter's, and one day, her heart in her mouth, she asked him: "What do you do in order to bilocate?"

Salarrué only laughed.

"I don't believe that you can appear in somebody else's house while you're really here all the time." Luisa squirmed with embarrassment and held her breath. She was twelve years old at the time and was passing through her scientific, materialist phase.

"Would you like me to give you a demonstration sometime?" Salarrué gave her an affectionate smile.

Luisa shook her head firmly and went out to the patio to play with her friends.

Years later, while she was combing her hair at her dressing table one night—there wasn't the slightest breeze at the time—a book suddenly fell from her bookcase onto the floor: it was Salarrué's *Cuentos de barro.*

# AND THIS RIVER POEM
## (1988)

*Translated from the Spanish by*
*Margaret Sayers Peden*

## Mater Potens

Today the morning began
with your eyes sparkling
in the mirror
your heavy-lidded tenderness
entangled in my eyes
ran up and down my skin
I opened my arms
like yours
uplifting my heart
with your fingers
I gathered bread crumbs
from the tablecloth
I made a lyre
a dog
a snail shell
the obstinate verses returned
to harass me
and for a long time I forgot you
I shook the rugs
remembered the daughter
who will soon be a mother
deciphered some dreams
listened to the leaves
dying of cold
and sat down to play
a game of solitaire
you put the jack
on the black queen
I leafed through your memories
like an open album:
faces I scarcely saw

in faded photographs
from my childhood
I smiled
you smiled
you asked questions
about me
about you
about my daughters
the questions became jumbled
I got up a sleepwalker
you led me to the mirror
your anaconda eyes
once more fixed on me
my anaconda eyes
on the one who will soon
be initiated
wanting to captivate her
hypnotize her
wrap her in the length of my embrace
of all my coils.

# Death Leap

*To Eraclio Zepeda*

It drifted down toward the floor
spiraling down
I thought it was a feather
the detached wing
of some butterfly
It was only a scrap of paper
that blew in through my window
your piece of paper
a coded message
I was unable to decipher.
Often in Paris the postman
delivered to me
your papers from Prague:
Cuscatlán recipes
smelling of *loroco*
and cinnamon.
Later
now in Havana
as I was lunching at the hotel
messengers arrived
bringing me things from you
butterfly wings
scribbled with signs
that I was not able
to understand.
I stumbled into you
everywhere
I began collecting myths
things that really happened to you.
I pressed them
like purple petals

between the pages
of a book.
It was there the earthquake
let you escape
from prison
the coup d'état
that saved your life
the dangerous adventure
with your sister.
Little by little
I began to understand
I began to decipher
your hieroglyphs
you invited me to dance
giddy I accepted
we danced in Havana
in Mexico
in Chalchuapa
you led me
through labyrinths of leaves
dizzily we climbed
we descended
it was always the same step
like an act of love
the same step
did I dream it?
did you dream me?
I awoke with your death
brushing my lips
your papers began to crumble
on the astonished tips
of my fingers
your papers
began to disintegrate
their characters faded
vanished.

We never danced, Roque,
never looked
into each other's eyes
(although maybe
Chuang Tzu dreamt the butterfly
or was it the other way around?)
I can't remember whether in Mexico
or in Prague
as you were drinking beer
you told Eraclio
we had danced
that I showed you that step
that deathly leap.

# From the Bridge

I have stepped off at last
it has been hard to do
near the end of the bridge
I stop
the water flows below
a swift-moving current
sweeping residue with it:
the voice of Carmen Lyra
faces I loved
that disappeared.
From here
from the bridge
the perspective changes
I look back
toward the beginning:
the hesitant silhouette
of a little girl
a doll
dangling from her hand
she lets it drop
and walks toward me
now she is an adolescent
she pulls back her hair
and I recognize this gesture
stop right there girl
if you come any closer
it will be difficult to talk
Don Chico died
after seven operations
they let him die
in a wretched hospital

they closed Ricardo's school
and he died too
during the earthquake
his heart failed.
Do you remember the massacre
that left Izalco without men?
You were seven.
How can I explain to you
nothing has changed
the killing goes on every day.
It's better if you stop there
I remember you well at that age
you wrote syrupy poems
you were horrified by violence
you taught the neighborhood children
how to read
what would you say
if I told you that Pedro
your best student
rotted in jail
and that Sarita
the little blue-eyed girl
who made up stories
let herself be seduced
by the eldest son
of her employers
and afterward sold herself
for two *reales*?
You've taken another step
you are wearing your hair short
and have textbooks
under your arm
poor innocent
you learned the consolations
of philosophy
before understanding

what there was to be consoled for
your books spoke to you
of justice
and carefully omitted
the filth that has surrounded us forever
you went on with your verses
searched for order in chaos
and that was your lodestone
or perhaps your sentence.
You are coming closer now
your arms filled with children
it is easy to distract yourself
playing the role of mother
and shrink the world
to a hearth.
Stop
don't come any closer
you still wouldn't recognize me
you still have to undergo
the deaths of Roque
of Rodolfo
all the countless
deaths
that assail you
pursue you
define you
in order to dress in this plumage
(my plumage of mourning)
to peer out
through these pitiless
scrutinizing eyes
to have my claws
and this sharp beak.
I never found the order
I was looking for
but always a sinister

and well-planned disorder
a prescribed disorder
that increases in the hands
of those who flaunt their power
while others
those who clamor
for a warmer world
one with less hunger
and more hope
die tortured
in the prisons.
Don't come any closer
there's a stench of carrion
surrounding me.

# Strange Guest

This guest is strange
this love
the more it deprives me
the more it fills me.

# I Want to Be Everything in Love

I want to be everything in love
the lover
the loved one
the vertigo
the breeze
the water reflected
and that white cloud
vaporous
uncertain
that covers us for an instant.

# The Woman of the Sumpul River

*For Karen*

Come with me
Let's climb the volcano
to reach the crater
we have to break through the fog
history is bubbling
inside the crater
Atlacatl
Alvarado
Morazán
and Martí
and all those great people
gambling with death.
Come down through the clouds
toward the scintillating
greens
*amate* trees
ceibas
coffee plantations
look at the buzzards
awaiting their feast.
"I was hiding in the river
for a long time,"
explains the woman
"a five-year-old boy
asked me to help him climb out.
When the army moved in
with all its savagery
we tried to get away.
It was the fourteenth of May
when we started running.
They killed three of my children

and when they took my man away
they took him bound and tied."

The woman is weeping for them
weeping in silence
with her youngest son
in her arms,
"When the soldiers came
I played dead
I was afraid the little one
would start to cry
and they would kill him."
She consoles her baby
in whispers
she lulls him with her weeping
she strips leaves from a tree
and she tells him:
look at the sun
through this leaf
and the child smiles
and she covers his face with leaves
so he won't cry
so he will see the world
through the leaves and won't cry
while the soldiers go past
following the trail.
She fell wounded
between two boulders
beside the Río Sumpul
she lay there not moving
with her baby
next to the boy
who wants to get out
of the water.
Ants were crawling
over his legs

and she covers them
with more leaves
and her baby smiles
and the other looks at her
without a word
he has seen the soldiers
and he doesn't dare speak
or ask a question.
The woman by the river waiting to die
the soldiers didn't see her
and they passed by
the children didn't cry
it was the Virgen del Carmen
she repeats silently
a buzzard slowly circles
above them
the woman watches it
and the children watch it
the buzzard flies lower
and doesn't see them
it's the Virgen del Carmen
the woman repeats
the buzzard flies
right past them
with its cargo of rockets
and the boys watch it
and smile
it makes two circles
three circles
and begins to climb
la Virgen has saved me
the woman exclaims
and she covers her wound
with more leaves
she has become transparent
her body blends with the earth

and the leaves
she is earth
she is water
she is planet
moist
oozing tenderness
wounded Mother Earth
who looks at that deep fissure
opening in her flesh
the wound is bleeding
the volcano is belching
furious lava
mixed with blood
our history
has been converted into lava
into an incandescent people
who blend with the earth
into invisible *guerrilleros*
who fall like
transparent cascades
the soldiers
don't see them
nor do the pilots
who are counting the dead
nor the Yankee strategist
who has faith in his armed
buzzards
nor do the five corpses
in dark glasses
who govern.
They are blind to the lava
to the incandescent people
to the *guerrilleros* disguised
as aged sentinels
to the child messengers
to the keepers

of safe-house shacks
for priests who lead
clandestine groups
of filthy beggars
sitting on the church steps
to keep an eye on the soldiers.
The woman of Sumpul
is there with her children
one sleeps in her arms
and the other walks beside her.
Tell me what you saw
the reporter says.
"I was hiding in the river
for a long time."

# Snapshots

*For Eliseo Diego*

My time is running short
I am almost
at the end of the corridor
amid the smoke
the tumult
the destroyers
that are being left behind
I discover other women
I once had been
and this me
the women I see today
with their burden of body
and nostalgia
is coming closer to another
who will jump from her niche
and look at us an instant
and will continue her journey
toward the darkness
that awaits us all.

# FUGUES
## (1993)

*Translated from the Spanish by*
*Darwin J. Flakoll*

# Savoir Faire

*For Erik*

My black cat doesn't know
he will die one day
he doesn't cling to life
as I do
he leaps from the rooftop
light as air
climbs the tamarind tree
barely scratching it
doesn't dread crossing bridges
or dark alleyways
or the perfidious scorpion
my black cat falls in love
with every cat he meets
he refuses to be snared
by a single love
the way I did.

# Ars Poetica

I,
poet by trade,
condemned so many times
to be a crow,
would never change places
with the Venus de Milo:
while she reigns in the Louvre
and dies of boredom
and collects dust
I discover the sun
each morning
and amid valleys
volcanoes
and debris of war
I catch sight of the promised land.

# Letter to an Exile

My dear Odysseus:
It is no longer possible
my husband
that time goes flying by
without my telling you
of my life in Ithaca.
Many years have gone by
since you left
your absence weighs
on your son
and me.
My suitors began
to fence me in
they were so many
and so tenacious in their flattery
that a god, taking pity
on my anguish,
advised me to weave
a subtle
interminable cloth
that would serve
as your shroud.
If I finished it
I would have to choose
a husband without delay.
The idea captivated me
at sunrise I set about weaving
and I unwove during the night.
my heart yearns for a youth
as handsome as you when young
as expert with bow and lance

our house is in ruins
and I need a man
who knows how to rule it.
Telemachus is but a babe
and your father decrepit.
It is preferable, Odysseus,
that you don't return.
Of my love for you
not even embers remain.
Telemachus is well
never asks for his father
it would be better
if we gave you up for dead.
I know from strangers
about Calypso and Circe.
Seize your chance, Odysseus,
if you choose Calypso
you'll regain lost youth
if Circe is the chosen one
among her swine
you'll reign supreme.
I hope this letter
does not offend you
don't invoke the gods
it will be in vain
remember Menelaus
and his Helen
For that mad war
our best men
have lost their lives
and you are where you are.
Don't return, Odysseus,
I beg you.

Your discreet Penelope.

# Malinche

Here I am
in the defendant's seat
you call me traitor
whom have I betrayed?
I was still a child
when my father—
my stepfather really—
fearing his son
would not inherit the lands
that were mine
took me to the south
and gave me to strangers
who did not speak my language.
I grew up in that tribe
serving as a slave
and the white men arrived
and they gave me to the whites.
What do you mean
by the word *treason*?
Was I not the one betrayed?
Which of my people defended me
when I was raped by the first white man,
when I was forced to kneel
and kiss his phallus,
when I felt my body sundered
and with it my soul?
You demand that I be loyal
even though I've been unable
to be loyal to myself.
Before I flowered
my love withered:

a child in my womb
who never saw the light.
How did I betray my homeland?
My homeland is my people
and they abandoned me.
To whom am I responsible?
To whom?
Tell me.
To whom?

# Hecate

I am the virgin
the woman
the prostitute
I am the salt
the mercury
the sulfur
I am heaven
and hell
I am the earth
you see me illuminated
maternal
Don't trust me
I can consign
you to darkness.

# Packing My Bags

*The barbarians are due here today.*

It's time to think
about my baggage
the suitcase is tiny
my perfumes won't fit
nor my necklaces
much less my books.
What will I take with me
to the other side?
Naturally the first
lightning bolt
that kindled our love
I'll also take
the razor glance
of that child
it wasn't for me
nor for anyone
blindly it grazed me
and opened this wound
that will not close.
I must be selective
in my memories
carefully compressing
those I pack
and out of self-compassion
abandoning the rest.
I will take with me
of course
the afternoon in Cahill's Tavern.
I told you about Sandino

and Farabundo
and you didn't understand
but wanted to learn
and little by little
we wandered into
the Halls of Los
and you were William Walker
and I Rafaela Herrera
and what was I doing
amongst the barbarians of the north
who invaded us
invade us now
and will invade again?
What was I doing
far from Izalco
far from my homeland?
And the night kept falling
quietly
and we were there inside
penetrating ever more deeply
trapped by our pasts
by our futures
and your tongue is foreign
I barely understand you
what am I doing here?
But I look at you and know
that you will be my man
and you still don't know it
and I stifle a laugh
and don't say anything
I choke down words.
It's impossible, I think,
what am I doing here
so far from my country?
And a tremor seized me
when I crossed the threshold:

my first earthquake
erupting in my Jurassic strata
and I encountered the mother
the children
the brother
Persephone
and Kali
and Tlaloc
and the night kept falling
quietly
on the empty bottles
and the glasses
and the waiter told us
it was closing time
and I walked out squeezing your hand
it was the first tremor
the first tidal wave
of the blind throbbing
that never abandons me.
You were the fish
slapping the water
with your tail
engendering these concentric circles
that open
expand
disperse:
waves that break
on my farther shore.

# THRESHOLDS
## (1997)

*Translated from the Spanish by*
*Darwin J. Flakoll*

# I. The Ceiba

How to forget that morning
when butterflies swarmed over my breast?
One lit on my hand
I could have closed my fingers
and trapped her
but she flew
she flew.

Years earlier
advancing hesitantly
over the chocolate tiles
Rilke vibrating in my hands
the hibiscus and jasmine
flowering
a phantasmal moon
behind the araucaria
sliced in pieces
by its branches
I believed I had entrapped poetry
but it flew
it flew.
It was in Glasgow
the crazed butterflies
only attacked me
children stared
wide-eyed.
Why? I asked myself
in bewilderment
why did they choose me?
It was the blouse
I knew

my blouse with autumn leaves.
But the miracle?
Who can explain the miracle?
Why did the butterfly
alight on my hand?
After that night
in the darkened patio of the house
with the moon watching me
through the araucaria
I began to conjure up words
began to invent butterflies
some sharper than others
but none corresponded
to the vision
vibrating in me.

I left my home left my people
my warm aromas
my dead.
Before my departure
my father
with clouded eyes
whispered in my ear:
"You won't return,"
he said
and gave me
a velvet-lined case
with a fountain pen
nestling in the satin.
"This is your sword,
princess."
Did he say princess?
No
I invented it
but he should have said it
because at that moment

I felt I was Deirdre
of the Sorrows.
"This is your sword,"
he told me.

Almost without noticing
I took destiny in my hands
time didn't matter
nor did space
the flavor of words mattered
my fountain-pen sword.

I left home
on the last day
I paused before all the mirrors
my image was strange
irregular
as if the mirrors had shrunk,
as if they distrusted me.
I left silently
without forgetting my Rilke.
I paused a long time
before the ceiba
before my protective ceiba
who shielded me
against the sun
while with other children
and stray dogs
and street vendors
we gathered beneath its branches.
There was no chaos
as in the labyrinths
of the marketplace
we could be ourselves
the ceiba covered us
sheltered us

brought us together.
Its roof was the map
of my homeland
like seeing sketched in the air
the restless map of my country.
I promised to return
to refresh myself in its shade
as often as I could.
The ceiba was quiet
not a single leaf
stirred
but I felt its benediction.
From its treeness
the ceiba blessed me.

## II. The River

Next came the River
the River
with its murmuring
its urgency
its ships coming
and going.

The margins of the River
were wide
and I knew it was another threshold
I had to cross.
How could I do it?
I was frightened
and yet I was not.
Alone facing the River.
The landscape was strange
the language foreign
I began walking through the city
nobody knew me
neither the streets
nor the houses
nor the faces.
Where was I going?
Was I still myself?
Was I giving birth
to that other self
I became?
The River before me
was the same
yet it wasn't.
It was river

it was challenge.
A toothless old lady
With a kerchief
knotted beneath her chin
approached me
there were furrows in her face
in her gaze.
"I am a beggar of miracles,"
she said stroking my hair
"can you give me one?"
"I had a dream a while ago,
I dreamt I was attacked by butterflies.
One lit in my hand."
"Thank you,"
the old lady said
she gave me a rose
and with rapid steps
she disappeared.

## III. Queen Bee

I sailed upstream
against the current
I sailed
jumped ashore
and began to wander
along perilous paths
my body impelled me
pulled me along
it wasn't that I had fled
from Santa Ana
from the ceiba
from the River
it was simply my body
dragging me with it.
One night
clad in cape
and sandals
I dreamt I was walking
through the sand
the sand was hot
and scorched my feet
and I scaled a crag
and saw the moon
and my skin shone
like the moon
and the moonlight
burnt into me.
I felt myself a queen bee when I woke
I buzzed
capered in the air.
I began to fly high

to descend
to feel myself besieged
by the drones
and I flew higher
I transformed into flame
and fluttered
it was the ancient millennial language
of the enamored body
the vertigo,
the pain
the piercing joy
I wept with my wounds
felt the sting
of the trap
the impact of the stone
thrown at random
but I also danced
with madness
with the winged specter
of death.
The five senses inflamed me.
The scent of basil was so strong
it assailed me while I slept.
The smell of oregano
of thyme
but also
the pungent smell
of male sweat
it was that celery odor
in which
I burnt
one night
at a dance
in a certain forbidden quarter.
And what can I say about blue
the electric turquoise-blue

of an iceberg
sprouting from the sea?
It was coldness
the abyss
the whale
blue conducted me
into the abyss
into the abysmal black of the whale.
Red on the contrary
red
was my childhood
the dress with frills
I loved
the hot midday
when my father and I
feeling deliciously guilty
shared the only watermelon.
Touch, smell,
taste,
ears and eyes
the five senses
seared me
inflamed me with love
catapulted me.
I thought
I could grasp poetry
with them
but it flew
it flew.

## IV. Merlin

And I kept traveling on the River
the River my road
I wanting to be a bridge
Suddenly
in some port
I glimpsed the wizard's cap of happiness
on the head
of a lone man
dancing amid the crowd.
I thought I recognized him
and drew near
he gave me a searching look
drew a wand from his sleeve
and sketched a lame bird in the dust.
"She is like you,"
he said
"if you learn to fly
you will have a better death."

Merlin
spawn of incubus
and woman
showed me how to draw
a mandala
how to bow to the moon
how to uproot myself
plant my foundations
elsewhere
and always be at home
but he also spoke to me of the word
the word that covers

and discovers
of its magic
its rhythm
its sound
of how you have to cradle it
hammer it
smash it.

A dark whirlwind
language
form and magic
the same
a whirlwind sometimes luminous
plethoric with origins
splendor
and music
and omens
a whirlwind
trying to open a path
and drag others with it
and peer into the abyss
and assail the stars.
The donkey expresses himself
with a crude braying
that makes us laugh
when perhaps we should cry.

The bird instead
incites us
to recall our future
we withdraw with its song
we withdraw with its flight
its clear-cut notes
propose
we polish words
into flashes.

The old man was a wizard
was implacable
he stripped me of my heavy garb
enwrapped me in words
and launched me on the search for poetry
I dove into the abyss
strange images invaded me:
Teotl
who created fire
Lilith
and Kukulkán
the sweet birds who wept
when a baby girl died.
I rose to the surface
and dove down once more:
skulls
pyramids
fissured wasteland.
I disguised myself as witch
jaguar
serpent
and kept on diving
and I found my *nagual*
but I told nobody the name of my *nagual*
and I will never tell it to anyone.

## V. The Tower

I came to the surface again
and You awaited me.
You were the magnet
bitten out by the moon
The horseshoe hitting me
in the womb
an itching blister
a call of the blood
to hoist sails
and cast off.
Merlin divined it
icy stars
shot from his eyes
icicles
from his lips.
He pulled his wand
from a sleeve
and with a single gesture
encloistered me
in an impregnable tower.
He transformed into scaly Fafner
guarding his prey.
Day and night
keeping watch
poisoning the air
with fiery belching.
He lined
the tower's walls
with mirrors
he wanted me unreachable
wanted me to preen myself

but I had been burnt
by Love
and he only offered me shards:
bits of glass
words
and mandalas
and moons.
Enwrapped in my silence
I saw my face repeated
a thousand times
I grew bored with my face
and shattered the mirrors.
One by one
I broke them all
I wanted to see you
you who were circling about me
calling out to me
summoning me.
A single window
at the top of the tower
not another hole
nor crack
nor so much as a loose stone
I gazed at my fragments
in the shattered mirrors
never the complete face
only fragments:
a clouded eye
a bit of lip
burning with your kiss.
The brush of your fingers
was still warm
on my skin
I could still scent
the wisps of smoke
that traveled

through your lungs.
I wept
screamed
pounced
I was a cat in heat
rubbing against the walls
a raging cat
inventing capers
I scaled the walls
with my claws
the trees lifted their crowns
to watch me
I peered out the window
and didn't see you
only Fafner shrouded with rancor.
I recalled your words
bunches of carnations
your words
beating against my eyelids.
"It's now
or never,"
you told me.
Your words
hammering in my ears:
"Now or never,
Now!"
The night was pitch dark
and I flung myself into emptiness
my mouth salty
with terror
but I flew
I flew.

# VI. Chalice and Fount

Suddenly downstream
this time accompanied.
Was it the Nile
the Mississippi
the Orinoco?
All rivers
my River
and I a swelling chalice
a potter
a noiseless vessel
gliding softly
sculpting another destiny.
Silence
darkness
fragmentary questions:
what color the hair?
how the hands?
I am astonished
at the miracle
at the swelling womb
creating form
effortlessly
quietly
my vessel growing
I am a nest
a giver of life
chalice
bridge
will it be a boy
a girl?
Will the skin be brown

the hair copper-colored?
I savor the moment
I am creating future
enchaining past
and present
an unexpected curve of the river
I love the world
seen from such angle
from that mirror haven
I love all mankind
and the beasts
and the birds
at night I converse
with the moon
I myself the moon
the full moon
inviolable
donor of life
potter.
I enter motherhood
with pain
my breasts began to swell:
fountains my breasts
distending
emptying
my daughter emptied them
while I cradled her
and the Great Mother cradled me
there is no space
nor time
we simply are
I concentrate on her ear
on the circumvolutions
of her ear.
How is it possible?
I ask myself

How was I able
to model perfection?
I feel myself omnipotent goddess
only my daughter
and me
she needs me
I need her
we are part of a plan
I cannot comprehend
nor do I need to.

# VII. The Coyote

I am navigating through time
not the River
but time
it is the wasteland
the desert
which dried my breasts
withered my womb
bent my body.
I sniff
as I trot along
I abandoned everything
I was abandoned
in the distance my daughter's cry
I am neither mother
nor daughter
I am a coyote
not a single cactus
nor a rivulet in sight
only repressed desires
dreams I myself
assassinated.
I must lock up
my memories.
Adverse solitude
surrounds me
I might have stayed with my people
accepted defeat
hopelessness
my wounds are painful
I roll in the dust
a dry wind lashes me.

In the distance
the far distance
the weeping of my daughter:
*"Duérmete mi niña*
*cabeza de ayote*
*que si no te duermes*
*te come el coyote."*
"Go to sleep my baby
my little pumpkin head
if you don't go to sleep
the coyote will eat you."
I keep on trotting
searching
tracking down the bones
of Vallejo
trak
trak
trak
tracking
Don Alex Sinegú
who read palms
predicted this drought.
An abyss beside me
in the depths
shards of broken glass
I turn about
at the edge of the abyss
I peer down
I withdraw
my image doesn't expand
the mirror swallows it
shattered fragments
of the mirror.
I flee terrified.
Suddenly a flowering cactus
I approach cautiously

a red flower
I remember the hibiscus
in the patio of my home
but this joy
is mine
mine alone
I can't share it.
Nostalgia pounces
I bark at it
entangle myself in roots
remember the old beggar lady
who offered me a rose
and I keep going
sniffing
trotting
tracking
a rabbit runs past me
will I have the same courage
for the next leap?
A bone at last
and another
and another
bones scattered
in the dust
I push them
gather them together
patiently gather them
a heap of bones
before me
dry white bones
that have lost their aroma
a mound of bones I sing to
the desert air
sponges up my song
and returns it in echoes.
I keep on singing

conjuring
until I sense the gaze
of the moon
and I lift my muzzle
and howl at the moon.

# VIII. The Crow's Eye

I am the crow's eye
the persistent eye
scanning
fugitive instants of my time.
I dominate space
with my wings
dominate the time
granted me
the brief bowstring
tensing
between birth
and death.
The past is my time
I am the arrow
triggered by the past
I must recover it
run through memories
with my eyes:
Izalco in the distance
smoke boiling up from the crater
the volcano belching
flaming
belching
spewing boulders
from its maw
orange-red rocks
rolling down its flanks
leaping
thundering down the slope
while the volcano weeps ashes
and I avoiding the smoke

detour to the plaza.
A fine rain
of ashes
white cotton tunics
crammed into the plaza
they are the men of Izalco
and their sons
wiping their faces
with kerchiefs
*traca—traca—trac*
the stammerer
the tunics crumple
dozens
hundreds of tunics
falling
writhing
remaining immobile.
Some are still walking
avoiding the cadavers
waiting their turn
walking on tiptoe
to avoid stumbling
against the dead.

A boy hand in hand
with his father
a child who doesn't understand
and gazes wide-eyed.
I beat my wings
and fly away
fly away.
The poet's sob reaches me
his unmistakable voice:
*Spain, take this chalice from my lips*
and I am in Guernica
in Bilbao

Madrid
I fly over the ruins of Guernica
mothers shrieking
dust rising from the ruins
dust like ashes
chimneys in Auschwitz
in Belsen
in Buchenwald
vomiting ashes
black smoke
and the ashes
of Jews who burn
and are consumed
years
decades of ashes
clinging to the faces
to the polished autos
of the Nazis
who seek in vain
to immolate a people
and like a flower
wear the death's head
in their lapels.
Why should I still care
for this planet?
The era of progress
was born in Hiroshima
with the atomic bomb in Hiroshima
with the orange mushroom
flowering in a thousandth
of a second
leaving the shadows of its victims
engraved on the remaining walls.
Thousands of dead
in Hiroshima
thousands

and thousands of living beings
transformed into ashes
into spirals of ash
into flames discharging
in the wind
the kingdom of death
here on earth
the dull droning of death
one sixth of August
in the morning.
I fly aimlessly
the small Vietnamese girl
enwrapped in flames
I fly higher
waiting
Jews persecuting Palestinians
Serbs decimating Muslims
piles of cadavers
blocking the roads
in Rwanda
tribal drums
tam-tamming
I alight on a tree
the forest is gone
a few rachitic trees
survive
an acid rain falls on the trees
poisons rivers
poisons the seas
the earth is ill
I scan the horizon
fugitive rays
of hope
of love
of courage
contagious rays

keep sparkling
despite the rain:
the revolution of carnations
in Lisbon
of students in Cuba
in Paris
Nicaragua
the lone Chinaman
with briefcase
confronting the column of tanks
in Peking
the Beatles
their songs
John Lennon preaching
"make love
not war."
I start the return flight
nothing has changed
nothing:
squadrons of death
bombardments
misery
Tlatelolco
Sumpul
expendable children.
My eyes cloud over
the landscape clouds
massacres in El Mozote
in Tenancingo
in Wiwillí
the dust of your streets
Tenancingo
into an exhalation of death
has turned.
Where have all the flowers gone?

## IX. The Butterfly

The ceiba no longer exists
they cut down my ceiba
the mirrors shattered
I dried my River
and the moon hid itself.
I am empty of desires
my sword rests
in its satin case.
Why now?
why
does poetry come to taunt me?
She entered by the window
poised in my hand
I gazed at her with nostalgia
pursed my lips
and with a breath
sent her on her way.

# SAUDADE
## (2000)

*Translated from the Spanish by*
*Carolyn Forché*

# Searching for You

I went out searching for you
crossing valleys
and mountains
plowing distant seas
asking of the clouds
and the wind your whereabouts
it was all useless
useless
you were within me.

## Saudade

I wish I could believe
that I will see you again
that our love
will bloom again.
Perhaps you are an atom of light
perhaps your ashes barely exist
perhaps you will return
and I will be ash
an atom of light
or far away.
Our love
will never happen again.

# Give Me Your Hand

*Today I like life much less*
*but I always like living.*

—CÉSAR VALLEJO

Give me your hand
my love
don't let me sink
into sadness.
My body has already learned
the grief of your absence
but despite the blows
it still wants to live.
Don't go away
love
meet me in my dreams
defend your memory
my memory of you
that I don't want to lose.
We are voice and echo
mirror
and face
give me your hand
wait
I have to rearrange my time
until I reach you.

# What Will Our Meeting Be Like?

What will our meeting be like?
Both of us without bodies
without your gaze
without my lips
on yours.
Perhaps we will be
particles of light
attracting each other
searching for each other
and finally fusing.

# Artemis

You are the triple goddess
the triple moon goddess
who engenders
visions in me.
From far off you shoot
and I ascend
and descend
you carry me from light
into shadows
and again toward light
and toward terror.
You are the good mother
the one with multiple breasts
who nurtures everything alive
the hunter virgin
who wants to cross the horizon
the voracious destroyer
the force that leads
and transforms me.
Our flight is nocturnal
and we fly and we fly
Artemis
and I drink your milk
and we cross galaxies
and I nurse serpents
in my flight
and I cradle death
between my breasts
and death is alive
it shines
and I follow the flight of your arrow.

# Orpheus

Give me your song
Orpheus
your word
a lyre forged
with the cords
of my being.
I must descend
to the kingdom of the dead
and awaken my beloved
and bewitch him.

# Unfinished Rite

*To my mother*

They say death is a solitary thing
that we die alone
though surrounded by those who love us,
but you called out to me
and I was not there:
I didn't close your eyes,
I didn't kiss your brow,
I didn't help you cross
over to the other side.
I was far away
far from you who gave me birth
who nourished me
who trained my wings for flight.
I didn't fulfill the rite
I was far away
too far
and that is the sob that carries me off in waves
in domes
in caves
and can't escape
and follows me around in dreams
and smothers me.
Forgive me/free me
for I need
to howl, beat drums
I need a blow to the nape of my neck
an explosion
to rip this sob out of me
So I no longer need to call upon you
in these my desolate
verses.

# It Cannot

Sadness
can't cope with me
I lead it toward life
and it evaporates.

# CASTING OFF
## (2002)

*Translated from the Spanish by*
*Margaret Sayers Peden*

# Medea

Those are not tears
streaming from my eyes
only the dry sobs
that haunt my night.
I murdered my own sons
they whom I most love—
or do I love you more, Jason?
Jason's sons
his happiness
his pride
I was the avenging arm
I buried our dreams
dreams that danced
like joyful embers
shedding warmth upon my face.
Jason abandoned me
because of him, I killed them
Jason
Jason
Jason
I shout your name
I howl
I clutch my dead sons
to my bosom
I rock them
I sing to them
I have nothing left
nothing
only the serpents are left
the winged serpents
that pull the chariot

carrying me to my exile
exile more cruel
than death.
I murdered my sons
I see their shadows
growing before my eyes
my sons' bodies
their luminous bodies
defying oblivion.
I am left without their voices
without their games
without their loving play
I shall moan and weep forever
walking
and wandering
in the desert
my song is of death
and of triumph
I did it for you
Jason
I did it for your love
the love you gave me
transforming me into a goddess
until suddenly one day
you tore me out by the roots.

# Francesca's Lament

*There is no greater sorrow than to remember*
*happy times in misery.*

—DANTE, *THE INFERNO,* CANTO 5

We were entrapped by love,
we broke the rules
and were dragged down to hell
upon a light wind.
Through black clouds
whirlwinds
storms
the wind bears us
punishes us
allows no truce.
I travel close beside him
my Paolo
I am chained to his side
we are one shadow
one cry
we are whipped
against one another
bound, unable to part.
Love is not to blame
love has no rules
someone who never loved
imagined this game
and callously flung us
into eternal agony.

# It's Time Now to Give Up

It's time now
to give up,
my exhausting,
and exhausted body,
give me the right to escape.
There was a time I loved you
you were fresh
entertaining
mischievous.
I feel sorry for you
you are bent and stooped
and you creak with every step
you're stiff
gaunt
and you've grown a belly
but despite your ills
and your quiet moans
you still want to live.
That love for life
that inflames you
does not let you
leave me.

# Lilith

You freed yourself, Lilith,
you left Paradise
in order to found your line
you never wanted to be
the subservient wife of
that boring Adam
you defied the void
you invented laughter
you were alone
alone
tirelessly seeking
your fate
from the depths of your anguish
rose your laughter
you danced beneath the moon
a dance without shame
and you laughed
laughed
you raked the universe
with your laughter.
The moon blushed
and cradled you in her bosom
you knew at that instant
that you were a fallen angel
and for the first time
you felt God
within you.

# My Cat

*For Sabrina*

How I envy my cat
who never suffers from insomnia
she sleeps on the sofa
on the floor
and if a noise wakes her
her eyes open, barely,
and then close again.
I am seduced by her idleness
her lightness
her poise
she bows to no one.
She wakes very slowly,
my cat, does her yoga,
starts toward me
closer, closer,
and rubs against me.
I stroke her
she scratches me
and skitters away with a leap.
She loves me?
She loves me not?
Mysterious is my cat
and I shall never know.

# I Must Let You Go

You, too,
I must let go
I must relieve you of the weight
of my mourning
leave you, finally, alone
with your enigma.

# MYTHS AND MISDEMEANORS
# (2008)

*Translated from the Spanish by*
*Maya Flakoll Gross*

# Mary Magdalene

I loved you Jesus,
I did
and you also loved me,
among all the faces
you looked for me
you wanted me near.
Your voice seduced me
the serene passion
of your words
I felt your flesh tremble
I felt the man tremble
when I anointed your body
with perfumes
and I washed your feet
with my hair.
I could have bewitched you
but I didn't
your look stopped me
your renunciation
among all men
you were the one
and I don't want to heal
from this love.

# Gaia's Monologue

I was born in the blink
of the light
the rain protected me
and the chaos of volcanoes flowed
the trees
the rivers
and the rivers ran
and the lakes appeared
and the seas
and I danced naked among the waves.
The wind
a wind from the north
enveloped me
made love to me
and I gave birth to giants
of a hundred hands
and Cyclops
and gods.
I am the keeper of life
and death
all my children
come back to me
I call them
I ward them off
I hide them in my breast
I feed off their bones
and they revive.
I am mother earth
a dark mother earth
I still keep the innocence
I had at birth

and look upon the universe in wonder.
I listen to the universe
I listen to it day and night
and my love is reborn.
I love it in the thunder
and the sun
in the galaxies
in every silent stone
in every flight.

# Phaëton (Son of the Sun)

At last, Father,
at last
I am in your carriage
there is no respite
dawn opens
its rosy doors
the stars fade
the horses are oiled
the required hours
I am the owner
of my father's carriage
of his four steeds
of fiery manes
and light steps
I hold between my hands
the hasty reigns
the steeds neigh
and they rise
cutting the air
apart.
Thank you again
Father
you gave in to my pleas
you regretted
your solemn promise
your face
was bathed in tears
your hands trembled
in the last embrace.
I will return triumphant
you oiled my skin

with magic potions
you wrapped my hair
with rays of light
and stooped you entered
your palace
don't despair
Father
because of you
your strength
your promise
I am the happiest
of mortals.

To look at the sea
from this height
is daunting
the road isn't easy
my father warned
the first part
is steep
then come
the slopes.
Give up your wish
Phaëton
what you want
is not for mortals
you will encounter
savage animals
the Centaur's bow
will be waiting
the Lion's jaws
Scorpio's pincers
and the horns of Taurus.
They fly
the horses fly
I never knew their names

it's not easy to lead them
I'm losing strength
the carriage jumps
in the air
my knees
shake with fear
Scorpio
threatens
with its
lethal poison
the reins escape me
the horses go off the track
why, Father,
why?
My bones will lie
in a foreign land
darkness
light
darkness
flashes of light
the clouds evaporate
the heat is fierce
my hair is on fire
the universe burns
you shouldn't have let me
I reproach you
Father
because of you
your weakness
your solemn
offer
I am the unhappiest
of mortals.

# Prometheus Bound

Dawn will not dare see the day
the ocean roils through storms
of black painted skies
the wind lashes
against my body
it lashes
and drives me mad
the time is near
I wake from my sleep
to the sound of wind
the eagle is close
I can't hear the beat
of her wings
but I sense she's near
and soon the horror
will start again.
Each day waiting
for the infallible eagle
I know by heart
the spark of her eyes
the head that tilts and slowly
with her beak
gnaws at the center of my entrails
here she comes
I sense her
not thunder
or wind
will stop her
my torment begins
who will rid me
of this fear

this pain?
The waves
have soaked my body
my wounds will sting
with salt
an eternal wait
an anguish
without end
my knees are trembling
I want to melt into the rock
that holds me
my only friend
my only witness
it feels my fear
and I feel it shiver
I caress the rock
with my fingers
with my nails
I sear it
day by day
this torture
the eagle will not relent
until the sun goes down.
Slowly slowly
through the night
my wounds begin to heal
dreamless sleep
without the chains
or the urgency
of lifting my arms
up to the heavens
and howl.
Damned be Zeus
and his court
I don't regret
stealing fire

for mankind
they will do wonders
and confront the gods.
I feel more human
than divine
here she comes
here she comes
I can make out her wings
what could be worse
the waiting
or the bird's beak
in my bowels?

# Phaedra

Hanging from the threshold
they will find
my body
Hippolytus
I will die of desperation
because of my love for you
which was never returned.
Without your knowledge
I spied on you
you practiced boxing
and long jump
and you were naked
and I was confused
I made holes in the leaves of that myrtle
that grows in the temple.
I wrote you a note
confessing my love
and you ignored it
my vengeance will be cruel
I will write to Theseus
saying that you
his beloved son
had raped me
and I tore my tunic
and I screamed
and sobbed
asking for help.
I'll leave the note on the threshold
there is no way
he won't believe me
Theseus is a proud man

he won't accept dishonor
you'll pay with your life
for your contempt
and Theseus will be the guardian of our tombs
I will tell him to plant that same myrtle
on mine.
We could have
been happy
Hippolytus
no matter if only for an instance
I am still beautiful
and I love you
I love you
and I curse you
I curse your look
my hunter
my charioteer
your arms and your legs
and your polished torso.
I love you with passion
and again I curse you
I love you with the rage
of a blind man's eyes
that will never see the light.

# Judas

Why Judas
why
did you betray him
with a kiss?
Why not
with an accusing finger
or a gob of spit?
With a kiss
you sealed the treason
and went mad
Judas
you ran to the rope
of your gallows
because a kiss is love
and you loved him.
In this abysmal night
of infamy
your image shines
and I forgive you
Judas
because I felt
your love.

# Judith

*To the memory of Nora Astorga*

At last between my hands
Holofernes
your bloody head
between my hands
your head a torch
stained with blood
that with your own sword
I sliced.
You believed my lies
they flattered you
we made love
and you slept.
I did it in cold blood
and I would do it again.
From these age-old
stone stairs
I behold my city
my pale Betulia
covered in stars.
Your time is up
General
you will never feel
the intoxication of power
your downfall was dull
without battles
without wails
without clamor
my hands are red
and your blood flows
over the silent stones.
I'm not boasting

Holofernes
It wasn't I
who did it
it was my people
my people
my people changed me
into an instrument
and took their vengeance on you.

# Isis

Where my love
my husband
my brother
where did Seth throw
your mutilated body?
What will we do
without your voice
without your kindness?
You are the fountain of life
king of light
and darkness
let me find you
let me pick up
the fragments of your body
one by one.
Osiris
gentle Osiris
who but you
will make the just and pious
come back to life
and the Nile overflow
to feed the earth?
Don't forsake us Osiris
I shall travel with Horus
our son
to the boundaries of earth
and I will search the air
and I will search the seas
and I will descend the Avernus
I must find you Osiris
I will hide you again

my love
Horus and I will be the guardians
of your body
and Seth
your loathsome brother
usurper of the throne
who dismembered your body
will never know
where you lie
and again like the wheat
you will be reborn.

# OTHERNESS
## (2011)

*Translated from the Spanish by*
*Maya Flakoll Gross*

# Sailing Away

*For Bud*

How difficult to be me
my days are spent
and I remain blind
deaf
without knowing
where to search.
I only know I loved you
I was your harbor for an instant
you sailed away
and as life does
you left forever.

# Daphne

I have taken root
become a laurel
because I rejected
the yoke of love.
My trunk stands still
but if the wind blows
my branches shudder
and I sing
and the leaves begin to dance
and the wind is aroused
and follows them
and the leaves shake
with more spirit
they want to dance
and flee
they come off me
and then I howl
and they fall bewildered
on the ground
and I relive the instant
in which I suddenly
stopped running
I became a laurel
and buried my madness
forever.

# Selene

*For all of life is a dream
and dreams are only dreams.*

—PEDRO CALDERÓN DE LA BARCA

Sleep, Endymion,
sleep
I will not wake you
with my kisses
let me look at you
and tell you
of my odyssey
your half-closed eyes
are lost
but I know you listen.

May Apollo forgive me
no one can match your beauty
your mask is perfect
but frozen
my eyes are locked
in your empty eyes
your face is a void
and it all starts
to fade away.
Let me tell you
before your charm
darkens the memory.

Yesterday afternoon
I stopped at a harbor
and I saw the boats weigh anchor
and I said your name

of golden syllables.
It's not only your beauty
that I love
when I saw you in the cave
I loved the light in your eyes
your tenderness
the way you spoke
to your flock.
Why ask of Zeus
a never-ending dream?
To preserve your youth?
To be immortal?
Each time you wake
you grow older
and I love you so much more.
It is you I have only loved
but you don't love me
Endymion
you are like the beasts.
like the dog and the cat
like the wandering bird
who fertilizes flowers.
Fifty daughters
and I have never felt your caress.
Do you hear my lament?
I would like to see you
torn to pieces
raving mad
tormented
by your own storm
I would like to crush you
between my arms
suck you
change you into
a cracked urn
where tears escape.

For thousands of years
I have circled the earth
and nothing mattered
I looked and I didn't see
I heard and I didn't listen
but love came
it opened a breach
and I started to see
to listen
to surprise myself.
I have seen so many things:
starry skies
abysmal skies
that threaten to sink me
black holes
that vanish
swallows that fight
against the wind
cataracts that explode
and dream themselves
hurricane seas
the silence of the oceans
the desolate sadness
of the ice melt
deserts that are canvases
and are scorched
by the midday sun.

I was a witness to love
and death
I saw skeletons of children
mutilated children
who smiled
and winked at me
I saw bombings
rapes

fires
fugitives in trains
going nowhere
but I also saw faces
changed by love
I listened to flattering poets
celebrating my brilliance
I was confused by the wail of a child
coming into the world.
I saw daybreak
and I saw the sunset
I listened to birds
sing
and frogs
croak
I caught the wind
making love to the stars
I was surprised by its wrath against the sea
against forests
against fire
I saw lions
eagles
reptiles
none reaches the cruelty of man
but no one loves
as he does.

I wish you would love me
Endymion
your vanity absorbs you
and doesn't let you be
you look at yourself
you're empty
the earth is exhausted
and you don't care.
It's time you woke up

let your love flourish
in sleep
it's time you suffered
harvest your incautious
tears
and watch them grow green
in your silence.
Come with me in my watch
hold yourself to my horns
make love to me in the air
caress my breasts
the planet is about
to explode
and time is a circle
without eyes
and the void doesn't exist.

Your drowsiness angers me
your sterile vanity.
Sleep, Endymion,
sleep
I will nail my words to your breast
and the wound will open
where love awaits
and we will fly together
like splinters in the wind
until weariness
moves us apart.
Is life a dream?
There is no death
only steps
everything ends
falls
to be born again.

# Sister Death

Hurry up and come
sister death
my life is a cup
filled to the brim
that only
belongs to you.

# Testament

*To my children*

I leave you
a shaky
ladder
unfinished
with broken rungs
some rotten
and more than one
whole.
Repair it
raise it
climb it
climb it
until you reach
the light.

**Alvarado, Pedro de:** A Spanish conquistador who conquered much of Central America in the 1500s. Alvarado is famous for the cruelty with which he treated the inhabitants of the region.

**amate:** A tropical tree whose inner bark is used to make traditional handmade paper.

**ars poetica:** A Latin term meaning "art of poetry."

**Astorga, Nora:** A Nicaraguan lawyer, politician, and guerrilla fighter in the Nicaraguan Revolution of 1979.

**Atlacatl:** A legendary hero in Salvadoran history who led the resistance to the Spanish conquest in the 1500s.

**atol:** A hot beverage made from maize.

**Avernus:** A volcanic crater that the ancient Romans believed was the entrance to the underworld.

**Betulia:** An ancient Israelite city saved by Judith from the Assyrian general Holofernes in the biblical Book of Judith. Also spelled Bethulia.

**Candelaria:** A town in El Salvador.

**ceiba:** A large tropical tree.

**Chacmol:** A type of ancient stone statue depicting a reclining figure, used to collect blood offerings for the gods.

**Chalchuapa:** A town in El Salvador known for its Mayan ruins.

**Che:** The nickname of Ernesto Guevara, an Argentine revolutionary who helped lead the uprising that overthrew the Cuban dictator Fulgencio Batista in 1959.

**chicha:** An alcoholic beverage made with maize, pineapple, and cane sugar.

**chiltota:** A bird that makes a nest like a large sack hanging from a branch or wire.

**Chinchontepec:** The second highest volcano in El Salvador.

**Chuang Tzu:** A Chinese philosopher who lived during the fourth century B.C.E.

**chumpe:** Roast turkey, traditionally cooked in El Salvador with vegetables and spices.

**Cojutepeque:** A city in central El Salvador, the site of a prison where hundreds of gang members are held.

*Cuentos de barro (Tales of Clay):* A 1933 collection of short stories about the injustices suffered by El Salvador's indigenous peoples, written by Salvador Salazar Arrué (Salarrué).

**Dalton, Roque:** A Salvadoran poet and journalist active from the 1950s to the 1970s.

**dans le Metro:** French for "on the subway."

**Doré, Gustave:** A French artist of the mid-1800s known particularly for his engravings.

**El Mozote:** A village in El Salvador where Salvadoran armed forces killed more than eight hundred civilians in 1981, during the Salvadoran Civil War.

**Endymion:** A handsome young man in Greek mythology who was loved by the moon goddess, Selene. His youth was preserved by eternal sleep.

**Fafner:** A dragon slain by the hero Siegfried in Norse mythology. Also spelled Fafnir.

**finca:** A piece of rural land with a cottage or farmhouse, often used as a vacation home.

**Fourteen Families:** The richest families in El Salvador. According to legend, there is one family for every major volcano in the country.

**gachupín:** A slang term for a person of Spanish heritage.

**guayabo:** A guava tree.

**Guazapa:** A volcano in central El Salvador.

**Guernica:** A village in northern Spain bombed by Italian and German warplanes in 1937, during the Spanish Civil War.

**guerrillero:** A member of a group of guerrilla fighters, who operate in small bands behind enemy lines.

**Holofernes:** An Assyrian general beheaded by Judith in the biblical Book of Judith to prevent him destroying her city, Betulia (Bethulia).

**Horus:** An ancient Egyptian god usually depicted with the head of a falcon, said to be the son of Isis and Osiris.

**Hugo, Victor:** A French writer best known for his novel *Les Misérables* (1862).

**izote:** A shrub often planted as a living fence.

**jacintos, pascuas, and mulatas:** Hyacinths, poinsettias, and orchids.

**Jara, Víctor:** See **Víctor and Violeta.**

**Kukulkán:** A Mayan god depicted as a feathered serpent.

**La Fuente Grande:** A town in Spain.

**La vache qui rit:** French for "the laughing cow," a type of cheese.

**"Las Nubes" ("The Clouds"):** A coffee plantation high in the mountains of western El Salvador.

**Lemus, José Maria:** President of El Salvador from 1956 to 1960.

**Lilith:** A female demon in Jewish folklore. According to legend, she was Adam's first wife.

**loroco:** A tropical plant with edible flowers used in many Central American dishes.

**maestro:** A title of respect used for anyone who is highly skilled, not necessarily a musician.

**Malinche:** An Indian woman who served as an interpreter and adviser to Hernán Cortés during the Spanish conquest of Mexico in the 1500s.

**maquilishuat:** A tropical flowering tree.

**Martí, Farabundo:** A revolutionary leader in El Salvador who led workers and peasants in an uprising after the devastation caused by the eruption of the volcano Izalco in 1932.

**mate:** A tealike beverage brewed from the dried leaves of yerba mate.

**Mater potens:** A Latin phrase meaning "powerful Mother," one of many titles given to the Virgin Mary in the Catholic prayer the Litany of the Blessed Virgin Mary, also called the Litany of Loreto.

**Melpómene:** The Greek muse of tragedy.

**milonga:** A place or event where the tango is performed.

**Morazán, Francisco:** The first president of the united Central America in the 1830s.

**muchacho:** A young man.

**nagual:** A guardian spirit among Central American Indians, believed to reside in an animal.

**nances, nísperos, naranjas, zunzas, zapotes, plátanos, and jocotes:** Central American fruits.

**Osiris:** The ancient Egyptian god of the afterlife.

**Parra, Violeta:** See **Víctor and Violeta.**

**perros:** Dogs.

**pito:** A tropical tree whose flowers are cooked and eaten as vegetables and whose leaves are used for medicinal purposes.

**pupusas:** Small tortillas.

**quesos:** Cheeses.

**Salarrué:** The pen name of Salvador Salazar Arrué, a Salvadoran writer, poet, and painter active from the 1920s to the 1970s.

**San Andrés:** A site of important Mayan ruins in El Salvador.

**Sandino, Augusto Calderón:** A Nicaraguan revolutionary who led an uprising from 1927 to 1933 against the U.S. occupation of his country.

**San Miguel:** One of the largest cities in El Salvador.

**saudade:** Portuguese for "yearning" or "longing."

**siete de junio noche fatal bailando el tango la capital:** "June seventh, fatal night, dancing the tango in the capital." Possibly a reference to a disastrous volcanic eruption and earthquake in El Salvador on June 7, 1917.

**Sor Juana:** Juana Inés de la Cruz, a Mexican nun and poet of the 1600s.

**Sumpul River:** The site of a 1980 massacre in which more than six hundred civilians were killed on the banks of the river as they fled from the Salvadoran army.

**Taltelolco:** An Aztec city in the area of present-day Mexico City.

**Tenancingo:** A town in El Salvador heavily bombed by the Salvadoran Air Force in 1983, during the country's civil war, killing at least fifty civilians.

**Teotl:** In Aztec religion, the creator and father of life.

**Thanatos:** The god of death in Greek mythology.

**tiste:** A beverage made of cacao and corn.

**Tlaloc:** The god of rain, fertility, and water in the Aztec religion.

**Via Crucis:** Latin for "Way of the Cross," referring to Christ carrying the cross to his crucifixion.

**Víctor and Violeta:** Víctor Jara and Violeta Parra were Chilean singer-songwriters. Parra owned a Santiago café where Jara performed regularly in the 1960s and 1970s.

**Walker, William:** An American adventurer who led private military expeditions in the 1850s seeking control over part of Mexico and over Nicaragua. He was executed by firing squad in 1860 in Honduras.

**Wiwillí:** A town in northern Nicaragua, near the Honduran border. It was a stronghold from which the Sandinistas, left-wing revolutionaries, opposed the U.S.-backed contras during the 1980s.